LECTIN FREE DIET

Discussion and Mouth-watering Lectin-free Crock Pot Recipes

(Easy and Healthy Lectin-free Recipes for Beginners)

James Botello

Published by Alex Howard

© **James Botello**

All Rights Reserved

Lectin Free Diet: Discussion and Mouth-watering Lectin-free Crock Pot Recipes (Easy and Healthy Lectin-free Recipes for Beginners)

ISBN 978-1-990169-19-9

All rights reserved. No part of this guide may be reproduced in any form without permission in writing from the publisher except in the case of brief quotations embodied in critical articles or reviews.

Legal & Disclaimer

The information contained in this book is not designed to replace or take the place of any form of medicine or professional medical advice. The information in this book has been provided for educational and entertainment purposes only.

The information contained in this book has been compiled from sources deemed reliable, and it is accurate to the best of the Author's knowledge; however, the Author cannot guarantee its accuracy and validity and cannot be held liable for any errors or omissions. Changes are periodically made to this book. You must consult your doctor or get professional medical advice before using any of the suggested remedies, techniques, or information in this book.

Table of contents

PART 1 1

INTRODUCTION 2

CHAPTER 1: ALL ABOUT THE LECTIN-FREE DIET 3

CHAPTER 2: MAKING THE TRANSITION 12

CHAPTER 3: BREAKFAST RECIPES 17

Granola Cakes 17
Lectin-Free Granola 19
Pumpkin Spice Pancakes 21
Apple Pie Pancakes 23
Sweet Potato Pancakes 25
Banana Bread 26
Pumpkin Cranberry Muffins 28
Fruit Souffle 30
Lectin-Free Hash 31
Lectin-Free Sausage Patties 32
Breakfast Skillet 33
Eggs And Sweet Potato Hash Browns 34
Shepherd Pie 35
Kale Scramble 37
Lectin-Free Burrito 38
Cheese And Artichoke Quiche 39
Pumpkin Bagels 40
Coconut Banana Muffins 41
Apple Bread 42
Spinach Frittata 43

CHAPTER 4: LUNCH RECIPES 44

Celery Soup 44
Sausage Risotto 45
Chicken And Celery Fries 46
Sloppy Joe 47

- Ravioli and Pesto 48
- Enchiladas 50
- Baked Sweet Potato 52
- Bok Choy And Fried Shrimp 53
- Fettuccine 54
- Meatballs And Salad 55
- Coconut Chicken 57
- Arugula Salad With Sweet Potato 59
- Chicken And Cabbage With Apples And Cranberries 60
- Mushroom Mini Pizza 61
- Orange Salmon Salad 62

CHAPTER 5: DINNER RECIPES 64

- Spinach Salad With Steak 64
- Noodles With Broccoli And Pesto 65
- Squash Soup 66
- Sweet Potato Gnocchi 68
- Chili 70
- Instant Pot Chicken 72
- Cream Soup 74
- Taco Cups 76
- Stuffed Peppers 78
- Curry With Pineapple 80
- Flap Steak 81
- Chowder 82
- Pot Roast 84
- Salmon With Capers 85
- Squash And Thai Curry 86
- Chicken And Blackberry Mustard 87
- Fish Sandwich 88
- Chicken Pesto 89
- Meat Pie 90
- Turkey Wings 92
- Butternut And Chard Soup 93
- Garlic Pot Roast 94
- Meatballs 95

SLIDERS	96
BURGER WITH EGG	97

CHAPTER 6: SNACK RECIPES 98

STUFFED POBLANO PEPPERS	98
HUMMUS	99
MASHED SQUASH	100
PESTO WITH PARSLEY AND CILANTRO	101
SPROUT CHIPS	102
CABBAGE WEDGES	103
MASHED CAULIFLOWER	104
OVEN FRIES	105
BASIL PESTO	106
SAGE PESTO	107
BRAISED CARROTS WITH KALE	108
BEEF BONE BROTH	109
CAJUN GREENS	111
CHICKPEA TRAIL MIX	112
STEAMED ARTICHOKES	114
PORK STEW WITH PINEAPPLE	115
CHICKEN BONE BROTH	117
FISH BONE BROTH	118
TURKEY BONE BROTH	119
JICAMA FRIES	120

CHAPTER 7: DESSERT RECIPES 121

CASSAVA	121
BALSAMIC STRAWBERRY SAUCE	122
LECTIN-FREE YOGURT	124
GREEN SMOOTHIE	125
CHOCOLATE CHERRY CUPCAKES	126
INSTANT POT APPLESAUCE	128
STRAWBERRY SHORTCAKE	129
BLUEBERRY DESSERT	131
MUG GINGERBREAD	132
GINGER CAKE	133

- Mint Pesto 135
- Peach Cobbler 136

CONCLUSION 138

PART 2 139

INTRODUCTION 140

- What Is Plant Paradox And Is It Healthy? 140
- Where To Find Lectin 140
- Disadvantages Of Lectin 140
- Vegetables 142
- Protein 142
- Fats 143
- Carbs 143
- Condiments And Others 144
- Fish 146
- Diary 146
- Noodles 147
- Nuts 148
- Flours 148
- Oils 149
- Others 149
- Red Kidney Beans 149
- Casein A1 Milk 151
- Fruits: Out Of Season 151
- Fruits 152
- Pseudograins, Grasses And Sprouted Grains 152
- Pork 153
- Oils 153
- Milk Products 154
- Vegetables 154
- Starchy Foods 155
- Ingredients Substitute 155
- Prep And Cooking Guidance 156
- Rinse The Beans And Discard Soaking Water. 156
- Potato Optimization For Health Benefits 157

SAFE LECTINS	157
PEELING OF FRUITS AND VEGETABLES	157
USE PRESSURE COOKER	158

RECIPES 159

MORNING MEALS	159
CINNAMON PANCAKES- LECTIN-FREE	159
MEXICAN BLACK BEAN TACO CUPS	161
CHOCOLATE FUDGE TARTS- LECTIN FREE	163
YUMMY GINGERBREAD MUG	164
VANILLA MUG CAKE- LECTIN-FREE	165
LIME MOUSSE TARTS	166
SNACKS AND APPETIZERS	167
BAGEL THINS	167
VARIETY OF DIPS	169

LECTIN FREE-PARTY HUMMUS 169

VEGETARIAN LOW LECTIN HUMMUS	170
PARTY PESTO-3	171
GARLIC SALTED RAINBOW OVEN FRIES	172
DIJON SALMON CAKE	173
SWISS CHARD FRITTERS	175
SOUPS AND STEWS	177
MISO RAMEN SOUP WITH SHIRATAKI NOODLES- LECTIN FREE	177
ROMANIAN STYLE BEEF SOUP	179
OKRA STEW WITH GREEN CABBAGE- LECTIN-FREE	181
VEGAN CORIANDER AND LIME CAULIFLOWER RICE- LECTIN FREE	183
VEGAN SHIRATAKI ANGEL HAIR PASTA WITH CREAMY CHIPOTLE AVOCADO SAUCE- LECTIN FREE	184
VEGAN MUSHROOM CAULIFLOWER RICE RISOTTO- LECTIN FREE	185
DRINKS AND SMOOTHIES	187
AVOCADO SMOOTHIE BOWL	187
CLASSIC HOT CHOCOLATE	188
AVO NOG	189
SAUCES AND SWEET BITES	190
WARM GINGER BREAD IN A MUG	190

BLUEBERRY FOOLS LECTIN-FREE .... **Error! Bookmark not defined.**
SMOKY MAPLE BARBECUE SAUCE .... **Error! Bookmark not defined.**
HOMEMADE GRANOLA BARS- LECTIN AND GRAIN FREE ... **Error! Bookmark not defined.**

Part 1

Introduction

Luckily, it is extremely simple to remove the unwanted lectins from your body, all you have to do is watch what you eat. Unfortunately, it can be more difficult than you might expect to pick out the foods that have lectins in them as they are not always marked and some of the biggest offenders are hiding in plain sight. To help you navigate these tricky waters, the following chapters will discuss everything you need to know in order to get started off on the right foot with the lectin-free diet.

First, you will learn all about the basics of the diet, as well as the many cons, and a few pros regarding lectins. Next, you will learn about making the transition to the lectin-free diet, which should only take a few days as long as you do it properly. From there, you will find a host of recipes broken down by category to help ensure that, regardless of what your favorites are, you will be able to find something to enjoy within these pages.

There are plenty of books on this subject on the market, thanks again for choosing this one! Every effort was made to ensure it is full of as much useful information as possible, please enjoy!

Chapter 1: All About The Lectin-Free Diet

Lectins are a type of protein found in plants, and the occasional animal protein, that studies have shown contain a number of negative, as well as a few positive effects. Some of the biggest lectin offenders are foods like legumes, beans, tomatoes and whole grains. Lectins are a type of protein that help cells interact with one another more easily when present in the body in small amounts. Plants produce it as a means of keeping insects away and also to help them consume the nitrogen they need in order to grow properly.

This is a problem because when lectins build up in the body they can negatively impact it in a wide variety of ways including things like an increased risk of chronic disease or chronic indigestion. They are categorized as an antinutrient because they block the absorption of many nutrients. If you have ever had a stomachache after eating uncooked beans or other plant foods then this is likely the reason why. In fact, according to the FDA, consuming just four kidney beans raw can be enough to cause a wide variety of symptoms including diarrhea, vomiting and nausea.

Good ways to decrease the amount of lectin in your foods include
- boiling
- fermentation
- sprouting
- peeling
- deseeding
- pressure cooking

Slow cookers typically do not reach a hot enough temperature to remove lectins from the equation and thus, while they are a delicious and effective way to cook a meal, they are not the right choice for these purposes.

While lectins can cause a wide variety of negative effects when they are consumed to excess, they are not all bad. In fact, studies show that small amounts of lectins can actually help good bacteria live in the human digestive tract and do their jobs more effectively. Research has also shown that it can be useful when it comes to diagnosing and identifying various types of cancer. To that end, researchers are even looking at lectin as a potential way to slow down the rate at which cancer cells multiply. Research is also proving promising in regards to using lectin as a potential treatment for illnesses related to viruses, fungi and bacteria.

Lectin-free diet

The lectin-free diet was popularized by Dr. Steven Gundry, a former heart surgeon who has since switched his focus to supplement and food-based medicine. According to Gundry, removing lectins from your diet via a lectin-free alternative helps to reduce body weight while improving overall health in the process. It is important to note that the official version of the diet also requires that users purchase a proprietary supplement from Dr. Gundry so following the diet outlined in this book may not be as effective without it. With that being said, this book is **not** recommending going out and purchasing the supplement without doing your own research on its efficacy beforehand.

With that out of the way, the lectin-free diet is all about limiting the amount of lectin in the body to reasonable levels as a means of preventing inflammation from developing due to prolonged exposure. Chronic inflammation is known to lead to everything from arthritis, to cancer, to even death.

Inflammation is not all bad, however, as when it occurs naturally in the body, it can help the body defend against possible infection as well as heal cuts and wounds. If it continues for a prolonged period of time, however, it can lead to a host of illnesses and other negative effects (described in detail in chapter 2), some of which can cause serious long term consequences when left unchecked. Luckily, there are numerous easy ways to reduce your levels of overall inflammation including changing your eating habits which is where the anti-inflammatory diet comes into play.

As a part of the inflammation process, the body creates an increased amount of immune cells, white blood cells and a substance known as cytokine as a way to combat infection. There are two primary types of inflammation, the first is a short term variety that presents itself as swelling, heat, some pain and redness. This is the early phase of inflammation and the symptoms that it brings along with it are caused by the fact that additional blood is flowing to the affected areas in an effort to treat the issue as quickly as possible. This ensures that the troubled spot is protected from additional injury as the body works to fend off irritants, damaged cells, pathogens, viruses and bacteria. Without the inflammation process, even minor cuts and wounds would never heal properly.

On the other hand, chronic inflammation happens slowly over a period of months or years while outwardly presenting no noticeable signs of the ever-growing internal issue. This, in turn, creates a gradual shift in the types of cells that exist around the inflamed spot as the troubled area will be constantly in a process of destruction and rebirth, sapping bodily resources and slowly festering and becoming something much worse than whatever the initial issue may have been.

Risks of the lectin diet: The lectin-free diet is an especially restrictive diet plan which may naturally make it off limits to some people including children and women who are pregnant and nursing. Those who follow the lectin-free diet also often need to look into alternative types of nutrients as the lectin-free diet removes a variety of nutritious foods from the rotation as well. It can also be a difficult diet for vegans or vegetarians to follow as whole grains, seeds, nuts and legumes are all, more or less, off limits. As these items also provide much of the body's daily fiber, following the lectin-free diet in the long-term may also cause constipation if alternate types of fiber aren't substituted into the mix.

Foods to eat
- extra virgin olive oil
- olives
- avocado
- mushrooms
- celery
- garlic and onion
- asparagus
- cruciferous vegetables, such as broccoli and Brussels sprouts
- leafy, green vegetables
- cooked sweet potatoes
- A2 milk
- pasture-raised meats

Cooked tubers: Taro root, yucca and sweet potatoes are all excellent sources of vitamins and minerals due to the fact that their roots have strong absorption abilities, drawing minerals from their surroundings. They are also going to be some of your primary sources for fiber as many other common options are off the table.

Leafy greens: Sea vegetables, seaweed, fennel, parsley, endive, spinach, mesclun, kohlrabi and lettuce of all types are all chock full of nutrients and should be a staple of your diet moving forward.

Cruciferous vegetables: Brussel sprouts, cauliflower and broccoli are all great choices when it comes to vegetables that are lectin-free. Onions, mushrooms, celery, garlic and asparagus are all good choices as well. What's more, they are also full of polyphenols.

Avocado: While the avocado is a fruit, it is largely sugar free and is full of healthy fats and soluble fiber as well. It is a great dietary addition if you are looking to remove antioxidants from your body while loosing weight.

Olives and extra virgin olive oil: Olives, and thus olive oil, are full of vitamins and nutrients that are essential if you want to remain healthy while on the lectin-free diet. They are both a great source of potassium, sodium, iron, calcium, vitamin E, vitamin K, fatty acids and polyphenols. They are also known to directly combat inflammatory activities in those who are dealing with autoimmune disorders.

Foods to avoid
- A1 milk
- meat from corn-fed animals
- corn
- If grains are consumed, the plan recommends products made from white flour instead of wheat.
- grains
- fruit, although in-season fruit is allowed in moderation

- potatoes
- nightshade vegetables
- squash
- peanuts
- lentils
- peas
- beans
- eggplants
- tomatoes
- peppers

Legumes and beans: Beans are known to contain more lectins than any other food which means you need to do your absolute best to avoid lentils, peas, beans and any other legume and if you have to eat them, cook them in a pressure cooker first. Additionally, it is important to keep in mind that many legumes hide as nuts which means it is best to remove cashews and peanuts from your diet as well.

Grains: While much of the Standard American Diet is based on grains, the fact of the matter is that humanity as a species has only been eating grains for a relatively limited amount of time which means that, by and large, our bodies haven't caught up yet. As such, eating grain to excess can lead to a host of health problems as your body simply doesn't know what to do with it all. What's more, most grains contain high quantities of lectins which means that if you are going to eat flour you should go with white flour instead as it is devoid of practically everything, including lectin.

Squash: When it comes to remembering what fruits and vegetables to avoid it is important to remember that any vegetable that contains seeds is actually considered a fruit including zucchini, pumpkins and squash. The seeds, as well as the peels, of each of these, are full of lectins which means that if you must eat these things it is vital that you remove the peel and the seeds first.

Nightshades: Nightshade is the classification given to vegetables like eggplant, tomatoes, potatoes and peppers. The peels and seeds of these plants are all high in lectin which means that if you are going to eat them you make sure to deseed, peel and pressure cook them first. Fermentation is also known to reduce the amount of lectin a plant contains.

Corn: Corn is used to fatten up cattle and it has the same effects on humans, largely because it is full of lectins. To eliminate this issue, eliminate all corn, corn syrup and corn-fed meat from your diet, you are sure to start noticing a difference almost immediately.

Casein A1 Milk: While it may sound like a science fiction movie, the fact of the matter is that all the cows in Northern Europe started showing up with a specific genetic mutation a few thousand years ago. While likely caused as a reaction to some long-gone disease, the mutation also added a protein called casein A1 to their milk, which contains a lot of lectins. Unfortunately, most dairy products are made from milk from casein A1 cows, even if the milk is organic. The only way to avoid getting lectin in this fashion is to either stop consuming most dairy or to specifically purchase milk that has been obtained from unmutated cows, which are designated as Casein A2. Those who believe they are lactose intolerant are likely just reacting to the Casein A1 in their systems.

Ways to further reduce the lectin in your food
While sticking to foods that are low in lectin or are entirely lectin-free is a good goal to keep in mind, sometimes that simply won't be a possibility. When this is the case use the following tips to keep your lectin intake under control as much as possible.

Pressure cook trouble items: If you find yourself on a path to consuming quinoa, regular potatoes, tomatoes or beans, then pressure cooking them first will serve to get rid of a majority of the lectin these foods contain. This doesn't mean you can put anything into it and remove a lectin-free version, however, as the cooker won't be able to do anything about more stubborn foodstuffs like spelt, barley, rye, oats or wheat.

Remove seeds and peels: As a general rule, when following the lectin-free diet you are going to want to deseed and peel anything that can be deseeded or peeled. The part of the fruit or vegetable that contains the greatest concentration of lectin is always going to be the seeds followed by the rind, peel or hull.

White grains only: While you are going to want to avoid grains as much as possible if you do need to consume them always choose the white variety over the brown. While the public perception is that things like white rice and white bread are automatically unhealthy, the fact of the matter is that there are high quality versions of these items that are just as healthy as the lectin fueled alternatives.

Saving money while eating lectin-free
Much like any specialty diet, those who follow the lectin-free diet should expect to pay a little more for groceries than would otherwise be the case. With this being said, there are still plenty of things you can do in order to ensure that eating lectin-free isn't going to break the bank. The goal is not to focus so much on what you spend and instead pay more attention to when and how you spend which involves making three separate shopping lists.

Weekly list: Your weekly shopping list, perhaps unsurprisingly, is the list that you will be using most often. It should contain all of the items that you consume most frequently as well as all the things you need to make specific meals throughout the week. This is the only list that most people create which is why their bills are traditionally higher week to week. As you put together your extended shopping lists you will find that you will be able to cross more and more things off your weekly list as a result.

Monthly list: This is the list that you will want to make at the start of each month and it should mainly stick to the nonperishable or longer-term items that you may be running out of. These are the types of things that you will want to buy in bulk either through wholesale clubs or online retailers. Once you have a good idea of what types of items will always be showing up on this list you can then constantly keep an eye out for deals on them and stock up on the cheap. Great choices for this list include things like:

- almond flour
- French or Italian butter
- dried herbs/seasonings
- nuts
- unsweetened coconut milk
- stevia
- vinegar
- hot sauce
- frozen vegetables
- olive oil

Seasonal shopping list: This is a list you will only need to make a handful of times per year as it will involve seasonal items that you can stock up on at the beginning of the season and freeze for use for the next few months. This is also when you should shop for free-range fish and pasture-raised meat as buying in bulk here will say you hundreds over a three or four month period.

Chapter 2: Making The Transition

Once you have decided to make the transition to a lectin-free diet a try, there are going to be a few things you will want to do before taking the plunge, starting with a three day detox plan design to purge the excess lectin from your system once and for all.

Prepare your body: As your body has long since adjusted to the amount of lectin that is currently in your system, preparing it to exist in a low-lectin state will require a bit of work. One common den of lectins is processed sugar which has likely led to an increase in bad bacteria in your gut that thrives on it. If you have ever felt a craving for processed sugar or other bad foods then this is likely the reason why. Unfortunately, these cravings and the related mindset they have no doubt created over the years will only make it harder for you to start today.

Nevertheless, you must push them to the side and persevere if you want to start seeing serious changes sooner rather than later. Specifically, it only takes three days to start and you will then begin seeing a marked reduction in inflammation, a more balanced assembly of gut bacteria, weight loss and an improved sense of wellbeing.

Three Day detox
This three day detox will help you to remove a majority of the bad bacteria from your gut, making it easier for you to take full advantage of all the recipes in the following chapters by ensuring the transition is as quick and effective as possible. It is important to keep in mind that if you revert back to your old habits then the bad bacteria will return and you will have to go through the whole process from scratch once more.

This is not to say that you can't slip and eat something you know you shouldn't, after all, nobody's perfect, you will only really be in danger if you eat enough of the types of food you should avoid that the negative bacteria will once again feel right at home. While you can certainly skip the three-day cleanse and jump right into the diet proper, taking the time to purge your gut first will ensure you move forward with every possible advantage.

Getting started with the cleanse is simple, all you need to do to start is to say no to certain foods that are high in lectin. Specifically:

- Farm animal proteins
- Inflammatory oils
- Canola
- Soy
- Corn
- Tubers
- Roots
- Nightshade plants
- Soy
- Eggs
- Seeds
- Sugar
- Fruit
- Grains or pseudo-grains
- Dairy

At the same time, you are going to want to ensure that you have plenty of the following vegetables around. You are free to eat as many of them as you like. You can eat them cooked or raw, though if you are already dealing with gut issues or IBS then you will want to ensure you cook them first. Fresh or frozen vegetables are both acceptable as long as they are always organic.

- Mushrooms
- Sea vegetables
- Seaweed
- Algae
- Perilla
- Purslane
- Mint
- Basil
- Parsley
- Mizuna
- Mustard greens
- Escarole
- Fennel
- Butter lettuce
- Dandelion greens
- Endive
- Spinach
- Mesclun
- Kohlrabi
- Romaine
- Leafy greens
- Garlic
- Asparagus
- Okra
- Cilantro
- Hearts of palm
- Artichokes
- Daikon radishes
- Radishes
- Beets
- Artichokes

- Carrot greens
- Carrots
- Chicory
- Scallions
- Chives
- Leeks
- Onions
- Celery
- Nopales cactus
- Kimchi
- Raw sauerkraut
- Radicchio
- Cabbage
- Kale
- Collards
- Watercress
- Arugula
- Swiss chard
- Chinese cabbage
- Napa cabbage
- Bok choy
- Cauliflower
- Brussels sprouts
- Broccoli

Protein: While in the midst of the starter cleanse you will want to limit yourself to small amounts of pastured chicken or wild fish. You will want to split your protein into two, four oz. servings and consume one in the morning and one in the evening to ensure your body continually has everything it needs to run at maximum efficiency.

Fats and oils: During your cleanse you are going to want to try and consume an entire avocado each day. In addition, if you

need to cook with oil stick to the following choices that contain low amounts of lectin:
- Flaxseed oil
- Hemp seed oil
- Extra-virgin olive oil
- Walnut oil
- Sesame seed oil
- Macadamia nut oil
- Coconut oil
- Avocado oil

Chapter 3: Breakfast Recipes

Granola Cakes

Total Prep & Cooking Time: 75 minutes
Yields: 12 Servings

What to Use
- Salt (1 pinch)
- Vanilla extract (.5 tsp.)
- Cinnamon (1 tsp.)
- Almond butter (.3 c)
- Coconut nectar (.3 c)
- Chia seeds (2 T)
- Pumpkin seed protein powder (2 T)
- Coconut (.5 c)
- Hemp seeds (.5 c)
- Chopped mix nuts (1 c lectin-free)

What to Do
- Place a silicon muffin tray on a baking sheet and set to one side.
- Chop the nuts so the average size is about that of a popcorn kernel and place them in a mixing bowl. Mix in the chia seeds, protein powder, coconut and hemp seeds and mix well.
- Add the coconut nectar to a frying pan before placing the pan on a burner turned to a low/medium heat and stir constantly until it begins to bubble. Mix in the almond butter and continue mixing until it bubbles again.
- Mix in the salt, vanilla and cinnamon and stir vigorously.

- Add the results into the bowl of nuts and stir well to coat. It is important to complete this step quickly as the nectar will harden if it cools.
- Spilt the results into the muffin cups and fill each firmly.
- Place the muffin tray in the refrigerator for 60 minutes to cool.

Lectin-Free Granola

Total Prep & Cooking Time: 20 minutes
Yields: 10 Servings

What to Use
- Raisins (.25 c)
- Coconut oil (1 T)
- Maple syrup (2 T)
- Sea salt (.25 tsp.)
- Cinnamon (1 tsp.)
- Chia seeds (3 T ground)
- Pumpkin seeds (.25 c)
- Coconut (.25 c shredded)
- Almonds (.75 c slivered)
- Walnuts (1 c)

What to Do
- Ensure your oven is heated to 325 degrees F.
- Line a baking sheet using parchment paper
- Add the coconut oil to a saucepan before placing it on top of a burner turned to a high heat. When it is malleable add it to a mixing bowl.
- In the mixing bowl, combine all of the ingredients, save the raisins, in a bowl and mix well.
- Spread the results on the baking sheet in a single layer and place the baking sheet in the oven for 10 minutes. Mix halfway through to ensure it doesn't burn.
- Remove the baking tray from the oven and allow it to cool before adding in the raisins.

Lectin-free cereal

Total Prep & Cooking Time: 5 minutes

Yields: 1 Serving

What to Use
- Cacao nibs (1 pinch)
- Goji berries (1 small handful)
- Coconut flakes (1 small handful)
- Almonds (1 small handful)
- Walnuts (1 small handful)
- Pecans (1 small handful)

What to Do
- Add all of the ingredients to a cereal bowl and mix well.
- Top with A2 milk.
- Enjoy!

Pumpkin Spice Pancakes

Total Prep & Cooking Time: 15 minutes
Yields: 6 Servings

What to Use
- Coconut oil (2 T)
- Coconut sugar (1 T)
- Coconut milk (2 T)
- Apple cider vinegar (.25 tsp.)
- Baking soda (.5 tsp.)
- Eggs (3)
- Vanilla (.25 tsp.)
- Sea salt (.25 tsp.)
- Pumpkin pie spice (1 tsp.)
- Pumpkin puree (.3 c)
- Coconut flour (.25 c)

What to Do
- Add all of the ingredients to a mixing bowl and combine thoroughly using a hand blender. Continue to blend until all of the lumps in the batter have been removed.
- Add the coconut oil to a skillet before placing it on the stove over a burner turned to a medium heat. After the pan has warmed appropriately add in .3 c of the batter and shape it

using a spoon. Let each pancake cook about 2 minutes per side.

Apple Pie Pancakes

Total Prep & Cooking Time: 25 minutes
Yields: 18 Servings

What to Use
- Raw honey (4 T divided)
- Coconut oil (3 T)
- A2 milk (3 T)
- Salt (1 pinch)
- Nutmeg (1 pinch)
- Cinnamon (1 tsp.)
- Baking soda (.5 tsp.)
- Coconut flour (.5 c)
- Vanilla extract (1 tsp.)
- A2 Milk (1 c)
- Eggs (4)
- Cinnamon (2 tsp.)
- Apples (2 c diced)
- Coconut oil (1 T)

What to Do
- Add the coconut oil to a skillet before placing it on top of a burner turned to a medium heat and let it warm before adding in the cinnamon and apples. Allow them to cook about 8 minutes.
- At the same time, add the vanilla, honey, milk and eggs to a mixing bowl and combining thoroughly before adding in the salt, nutmeg, cinnamon, baking soda and coconut flour.
- After the apples have finished cooking, add in half of the apples to the batter and mix well.
- Add the remaining coconut oil, raw honey and 3 T milk to the skillet and stir while the oil melts. Remove from the burner and set aside.

- Add the coconut oil to a skillet before placing it on the stove over a burner turned to a medium heat. After the pan has warmed appropriately add in .3 c of the batter and shape it using a spoon. Let each pancake cook about 2 minutes per side.

Sweet Potato Pancakes

Total Prep & Cooking Time: 20 minutes
Yields: 6 Servings

What to Use
- Coconut oil (2 T)
- Eggs (4)
- Sea salt (1 pinch)
- Nutmeg (.5 tsp.)
- Cinnamon (.5 tsp.)
- Vanilla extract (1 tsp.)
- Nut butter (.5 c)
- Sweet potato (1 chopped, peeled)

What to Do
- Cook the sweet potato in a pressure cooker to remove as much lectin as possible.
- Add the sweet potato to a mixing bowl and mash thoroughly before adding in 4 egg yolks and the nut butter and mix well. Mix in the salt, nutmeg, cinnamon and vanilla.
- In a separate bowl, beat the egg whites until they are stiff enough to stand alone before adding them to the batter. This is important to ensure your pancakes come out as fluffy as possible.
- Add the coconut oil to a skillet before placing it on the stove over a burner turned to a medium heat. After the pan has warmed appropriately add in .3 c of the batter and shape it using a spoon. Let each pancake cook about 2 minutes per side.

Banana Bread

Total Prep & Cooking Time: 65 minutes
Yields: 6 Servings

What to Use
- Cacao nibs (.5 c)
- Raw honey (.5 c)
- Bananas (1 c mashed)
- Eggs (3 room temp)
- Coconut oil (2 T melted)
- Coconut flour (.25 c)
- Almond flour (.75 c)
- Sea salt (.5 tsp.)
- Baking soda (.75 tsp.)

What to Do
- Ensure your oven is heated to 350 degrees F
- Add all of the dry ingredients to a mixing bowl and whisk well.
- Separately, combine all of the wet ingredients and then mix the two bowls together. Use a mixer if needed to ensure batter is blended well.
- Grease a baking pan using coconut oil before adding in the batter and placing the pan in the oven for 45 minutes.

- You will know the bread is ready when you can stick a knife into the center of it and pull it out clean.

Pumpkin Cranberry Muffins

Total Prep & Cooking Time: 45minutes
Yields: 12 Servings

What to Use
- Orange zest (1 orange)
- Cranberries (1 c)
- Vanilla extract (1 tsp.)
- Palm shortening (.25 c)
- Raw honey (.5 c)
- Eggs (4)
- Pumpkin puree (1 c)
- Cloves (1 tsp.)
- Cinnamon (1 T)
- Sea salt (.5 tsp.)
- Baking powder (.5 tsp.)
- Baking soda (.5 tsp.)
- Coconut flour (.5 c)
- Tapioca flour (.3 c)

What to Do
- Ensure your oven is heated to 350 degrees F
- Fill a standard muffin tin with paper liners

- Add the spices, salt, baking powder, baking soda, coconut flour and tapioca flour to a mixing bowl and combine thoroughly.
- In a separate bowl, mix together the vanilla, shortening, honey, eggs and pumpkin and mix until it is completely smooth.
- Combine the two bowls and mix until smooth before adding in the zest and the cranberries.
- Add the batter to the muffin tin before placing the tin in the oven for 25 minutes. You will know the muffins are ready when you can stick a toothpick into the center muffin and pull it out clean.

Fruit Souffle

Total Prep & Cooking Time: 35 minutes
Yields: 2 Servings

What to Use
- Coconut oil (1 T)
- Mixed frozen fruit (1 c)
- Cinnamon (2 tsp.)
- Vanilla (2 tsp.)
- Raw honey (2 T)
- Eggs (4 room temp, whites and yolks separated)

What to Do
- Ensure your oven is heated to 350 degrees F,
- Add the fruit and coconut oil to a pair of large ramekins. Add the ramekins to the oven while it is preheating to melt the oil and soften the fruit.
- Add the egg whites to a stand mix and whisk until they begin to solidify.
- In a separate bowl, mix together the yolks, cinnamon, vanilla and raw honey.
- Combine the two egg mixtures and whisk briefly until they incorporate. Shoot for 5 seconds, do not over mix.
- Remove the ramekins from the oven and slice the fruit before adding in the egg mixture to each.
- Place the ramekins back in the oven for about 16 minutes.

Lectin-Free Hash

Total Prep & Cooking Time: 35 minutes
Yields: 3 Servings

What to Use
- Sage (1 T minced)
- Sweet potato (1 large, cubed)
- Coconut oil (2 T)
- Cinnamon (1 tsp.)
- Apple (1 cubed)
- Onion (1 chopped fine)
- Pancetta (6 oz. diced)

What to Do
- Add the pancetta to a skillet before placing it on top of a burner turned to a low/medium heat. Allow it to cook about 3 minutes before removing it from the skillet while retaining the fat.
- Add the cinnamon, apples and onion to the skillet and allow everything to cook about 7 minutes.
- Remove the ingredients from the pan and add them to the pancetta.
- Ensure there is still fat in the skillet before adding in the potatoes and letting them cook about 2 minutes before stirring well and then cooking another 2 minutes. Continue cooking and stirring until the potatoes have browned completely.
- Add everything back to the pan and mix in the sage. Let everything warm prior to serving.

Lectin-Free Sausage Patties

Total Prep & Cooking Time: 25 minutes
Yields: 6 patties

What to Use
- Red pepper flakes (.5 tsp.)
- Raw honey (2 tsp.)
- Oregano (1 tsp. dried)
- Basil (1 tsp. dried)
- Black pepper (1 tsp.)
- Chili powder (1 tsp.)
- Thyme (.5 tsp.)
- Sage (1 tsp. ground)
- Sea salt (2 tsp.)
- Parsley (2 tsp. minced)
- Onion (.3 c pureed)
- Turkey (1.25 lbs. ground)
- Pork (2 lbs. ground)

What to Do
- Add all the seasonings to a mixing bowl and mix well before adding in the onion, syrup and meat. Use your hands to combine thoroughly and then shape into 6 patties.
- Add the coconut oil to a skillet before placing it on the stove over a burner turned to a medium/high heat. Cook each patty about 2 minutes per side.

Breakfast Skillet

Total Prep & Cooking Time: 25 minutes
Yields: 4 Servings

What to Use
- Water (.5 c)
- Onion powder (.5 tsp.)
- Pepper (.5 tsp.)
- Salt (.5 tsp.)
- Homemade breakfast sausage (1 lb.)
- Coconut oil (1 T)
- Butternut squash (12 oz. cubed)

What to Do
- Add 1 T coconut oil to the skillet before placing it on the stove over a burner turned to a high/medium heat.
- Add the butternut squash to the pan and allow it to sauté for about 2 minutes.
- Add in the water before letting everything cook about 4 minutes or until the water has been completely absorbed.
- Move the squash to the sides of the pan before adding the sausage to allow it to brown. Do not mix the two until the sausage has completely browned.
- Mix all of the ingredients together and season as desired before cooking an additional 60 seconds.
- Serve hot.

Eggs And Sweet Potato Hash Browns

Total Prep & Cooking Time: 20 minutes
Yields: 2 Servings

What to Use
- Eggs (4)
- Sweet potato (1 peeled, skinned)

What to Do
- Ensure your oven is heated to 400 degrees F.
- Prepare a muffin tin by greasing it using coconut oil.
- Grate the sweet potato using a cheese grater and collect the shavings in a mixing bowl. Fill the muffin tin with the sweet potato shavings and press down well to create a crust.
- Place the muffin tin in the oven for 5 minutes, take care not to burn the sweet potato.
- Remove the tin from the oven and crack an egg into each section of sweet potato crust. Return the muffin tin back to the oven and let everything bake an additional 10 minutes.
- Let cool prior to removing from tin and serving.

Shepherd Pie

Total Prep & Cooking Time: 35 minutes
Yields: 4 Servings

What to Use
- Hot sauce (3 T)
- Avocado (.5 sliced)
- Cheddar Jack cheese (.3 c)
- Bacon (6 slices cooked)
- Pepper (.25 tsp.)
- Cumin (.25 tsp.)
- Chili powder (.25 tsp.)
- Paprika (.25 tsp.)
- Sea salt (.5 tsp.)
- Egg (1 beaten)
- Coconut flour (2 T)
- Cauliflower (.5 c grated)
- A2 milk (2 T)
- Eggs (4 beaten)

What to Do
- Ensure your oven is heated to 400 degrees F.
- Prepare 4 ramekins for use by greasing them with coconut oil.
- Add the salt, pepper, milk and eggs to a large mixing bowl and combine thoroughly. Add the results evenly to the ramekins and place them in the oven for 10 minutes.
- Remove the ramekins from the oven and allow them to cool before layering 2 bacon slices on top of each.
- In a large mixing bowl combine the pepper, cumin, chili powder, paprika, salt, cheese, egg, coconut flour, and cauliflower and mix well. Split the results into the ramekins and spread evenly.

- Brush the tops of the ramekins using coconut oil before placing them back in the oven for 20 minutes.
- Let cool prior to serving.

Kale Scramble

Total Prep & Cooking Time: 10 minutes
Yields: 1 Serving

What to Use
- Pepper (as desired)
- Salt (as desired)
- Coconut oil (1 T)
- Garlic powder (1 tsp.)
- Turmeric (1.5 tsp.)
- Kale (1 c chopped)
- Eggs (2)

What to Do
- Add the coconut oil to a skillet before placing it on the stove over a burner turned to a medium heat.
- Whisk the eggs in a small bowl and set aside.
- Add the kale to the skillet and allow it to wilt slightly before adding in the eggs, pepper, salt, garlic powder and turmeric.
- Let everything cook until the eggs reach your desired consistency.

Lectin-Free Burrito

Total Prep & Cooking Time: 15 minutes
Yields: 4 Servings

What to Use
- Black pepper (as desired)
- Sea salt (as desired)
- Gluten-free flour tortillas (4)
- Onion (.5 diced)
- Cheddar cheese (.75 c died)
- Eggs (4)
- Coconut oil (2 T)

What to Do
- Add the coconut oil to a skillet before placing it on the stove over a burner turned to a medium heat. Add in the onions and allow them to cook for about 3 minutes until they begin to brown.
- Add in the salt, eggs and cheese and scramble the eggs until they reach your desired consistency and remove from skillet.
- Warm tortillas in oven.
- Split ingredients in fourths between tortillas prior to serving.

Cheese And Artichoke Quiche

Total Prep & Cooking Time: 35 minutes
Yields: 6 Servings

What to Use
- Black pepper (as desired)
- Sea salt (.25 tsp.)
- Nutmeg (1 dash)
- Rosemary leaves (.5 tsp. ground)
- Cheddar cheese (2 c shredded)
- Eggs (5 beaten)
- Artichoke hearts (1 c chopped)
- Garlic (2 cloves minced)
- Red onion (1 sliced)

What to Do
- Ensure your oven is heated to 350 degrees F.
- Prepare a quiche pan by greasing it with coconut oil.
- Add all of the ingredients to a mixing bowl and combine thoroughly.
- Pour the results into the quiche pan and ensure it is even.
- Place the quiche pan in the oven and let it cook approximately 25 minutes. You will know it is ready when you can push a toothpick through the center and pull it out clean.
- Let cool 5 minutes prior to serving.

Pumpkin Bagels

Total Prep & Cooking Time: 35 minutes
Yields: 8 Servings

What to Use
- Apple cider vinegar (1 tsp.)
- Baking soda (.5 tsp.)
- Raw honey (1.5 T)
- Sea salt (1 pinch)
- Cinnamon (.5 tsp.)
- Pumpkin pie spice (1.25 tsp.)
- Vanilla extract (1 tsp.)
- Pumpkin puree (.5 c)
- Coconut oil (2 T)
- Eggs (3 beaten)
- Golden flax meal (3 T)

What to Do
- Ensure your oven is heated to 350 degrees F.
- Prepare a bagel pan by greasing it with coconut oil.
- Add the sea salt, cinnamon, pumpkin pie spice, golden flax meal and coconut flour to a large mixing bowl and mix well.
- Separately, mix together honey, vanilla extract, milk of choice, pumpkin puree, coconut oil and egg.
- Combine the vinegar and baking soda together and mix well before quickly adding the fizzing results to the egg mixture.
- Combine the two bowl and mix until smooth.
- Add the batter to the pan and ensure the space for the hole is clean.
- Place the pan in the oven for about 25 minutes or until the tops are browned and firm.
- Allow bagels to cool completely prior to removing them from the pan.

Coconut Banana Muffins

Total Prep & Cooking Time: 20 minutes
Yields: 40 minimuffins

What to Use
- Cinnamon (1 tsp.)
- Coconut oil (.5 c)
- Vanilla extract (1 tsp.)
- Bananas (4 mashed)
- Coconut (.25 c shredded)
- Coconut sugar (.25 c)
- Eggs (2)
- Sea salt (1 tsp.)
- Baking soda (1 tsp.)
- All-purpose flour (2 c)

What to Do
- Ensure your oven is heated to 350 degrees F.
- Add liners to two minimuffin pans.
- Add all of the dry ingredients to a large mixing bowl and combine thoroughly. Retain 1 T shredded coconut.
- Beat the eggs in a separate bowl before adding them to the dry ingredients bowl and mix well. Add in the rest of the wet ingredients and mix until the batter is sticky but do not overmix.
- Add the batter to the minimuffin pans before placing them in the oven for about 15 minutes.
- Top with remaining coconut prior to serving.

Apple Bread

Total Prep & Cooking Time: 80 minutes
Yields: 4 Servings

What to Use
- Organic cinnamon (1 tsp.)
- Coconut oil (.5 c)
- Water (.3 c filtered)
- Apple cider vinegar (1 T)
- Vanilla extract (1 tsp.)
- Apple (2 c diced)
- Coconut sugar (.25 c)
- Eggs (2)
- Sea salt (1 tsp.)
- Baking powder (1 tsp.)
- Baking soda (1 tsp.)
- All-purpose flour (2 c)

What to Do
- Ensure your oven is heated to 350 degrees F.
- Prepare a loaf pan by greasing it with coconut oil.
- Add all of the dry ingredients to a large mixing bowl and combine thoroughly.
- Beat the eggs in a separate bowl before adding them to the dry ingredients bowl and mix well. Add in the rest of the wet ingredients and mix until the batter is sticky but do not overmix.
- Add the batter to the pan before placing it in the oven and letting it cook about 65 minutes.

Spinach Frittata

Total Prep & Cooking Time: 40 minutes
Yields: 4 Servings

What to Use
- Salt (as desired)
- Pepper (as desired)
- Coconut oil (2 T)
- Cheese (5.3 oz. shredded)
- Bacon (5.3 oz.)
- Spinach (8 oz.)
- Heavy whipping cream (1 c)
- Eggs (8)

What to Do
- Start by making sure your oven is heated to 350F.
- Add the oil to a pan before placing the pan on the stove over a burner turned to a high/medium heat and let it melt before adding in the bacon and allowing it to fry until crispy before adding in the spinach.
- In a small mixing bowl, combine the heavy whipping cream and eggs and whisk well.
- Add the results to a prepared baking dish before crumbling the bacon and adding it, the cheese and the egg to the mixture and combining thoroughly.
- Place the dish in the oven and let it bake for approximately 25 minutes.
- Let cool 5 minutes prior to serving.

Chapter 4: Lunch Recipes

Celery Soup

Total Prep & Cooking Time: 30 minutes
Yields: 4 Servings

What to Use
- Black pepper (as desired)
- Sea salt (as desired)
- Coconut milk (1 c)
- Yellow onion (1 chopped)
- Water (2 c)
- Dill (.5 tsp.)
- Sea salt (1 pinch)
- Celery (1 bunch chopped)

What to Do
- Add all of the ingredients to an Instant Pot and mix well. Seal the lid and choose the option for soup. This will warm the soup for 30 minutes before switching to a warming mode for a few hours.
- Once the timer goes off select the option to manually vent the pressure.
- Add the ingredients to an immersion blender and blend well.
- Serve hot.

Sausage Risotto

Total Prep & Cooking Time: 30 minutes
Yields: 4 Servings

What to Use
- Coconut oil (1 T)
- Summer squash (2 diced, seeded)
- Onions (2 c sliced)
- Cajun seasoning (1 T)
- Water (3.5 c)
- Leafy greens (2 handfuls chopped)
- Rope sausage (1.5 lbs. diagonally sliced)
- Arborio rice (2 c)
- Bell peppers (1.5 c diced)

What to Do
- Add the spices and the salt to a small bowl and mix well before sprinkling over the top of the sausage and rubbing well.
- Turn your pressure cooker to a high/medium heat and add in the coconut oil and allow it to melt before adding in the sausage and allowing it to cook about 3 minutes.
- Add in the remaining ingredients and stir well before cooking an additional 3 minutes.
- Sir in the remaining ingredients and close the lid before selecting the option for high heat and full pressure. Let everything cook for 5 minutes before letting it sit for 5 minutes and letting the pressure release an addition 3 minutes.
- Add in the remaining seasoning and stir well prior to serving.

Chicken And Celery Fries

Total Prep & Cooking Time: 35 minutes
Yields: 6 Servings

What to Use-Chicken
- Olive oil (2 T)
- Black pepper (.25 tsp.)
- Salt (.5 tsp.)
- Chicken breasts (4)

What to Use-fries
- Black pepper (.25 tsp.)
- Salt (.5 tsp.)
- Olive oil (2 T)
- Celery (1.5 lbs.)

What to Do
- Start by making sure your oven is heated to 400 degrees F.
- Cut chicken into small pieces and place into a large mixing bowl before coating in oil and seasoning using spices. Let it marinate for a minimum of 15 minutes.
- While the chicken marinates, cut the celery into strips before adding to a separate mixing bowl, coating in oil and seasoning with salt and pepper. Shake well.
- Add the fries to a baking sheet and place them in the oven to bake 20 minutes.
- Broil the chicken until its internal temperature reads at least 165 degrees Fahrenheit.

Sloppy Joe

Total Prep & Cooking Time: 75 minutes
Yields: 6 Servings

What to Use
- Black pepper (as desired)Sea salt (as desired)
- Avocado oil (1 T)
- Pistachios (.25 c shelled)
- Water (.75 c)
- Chili (1 crushed)
- Paprika (.5 tsp.)
- Ginger (1 T minced)
- Garam masala (1 tsp.)
- Avocado oil (2 T)
- Garlic (1 clove minced)
- Avocado (1 mashed)
- Ground turkey (1 lb.)
- Avocado oil (2 T)
- White onion (.3 c diced fine)
- Cumin (1 tsp.)
- Apple cider vinegar (1 tsp.)
- Coconut milk (.25 c)

- Cilantro (1 handful chopped)

What to Do
- Add 2 T avocado oil to a skillet before placing it on the stove over a burner turned to a medium/low heat and adding in the pistachios. Allow them to cook about 4 minutes and set aside.
- Add 2 T avocado oil to a pot before placing in on a burner turned to a medium heat and adding in the ginger and garlic. Allow them to brown for 60 seconds before adding in the garam masala, water, mashed avocado, salt, paprika and chili. Allow the pot to simmer, covered while you complete the next steps.
- Add the remaining avocado oil to the skillet before adding in the cumin and onions and stirring for 5 minutes before adding in the beef and the chilis. Brown the meat completely.
- Add the skillet ingredients to the pot and turn up the heat to allow it to boil, removing the lid slightly to vent. Simmer for an additional 15 minutes on low/medium heat.
- Add in the pistachios, vinegar and coconut milk and mix well prior to serving. Garnish with cilantro.

Ravioli and pesto

Total Prep & Cooking Time: 35 minutes
Yields: 1 Serving

What to Use
- Parmesan cheese (.25 c)
- Mascarpone (.25 c)
- Coconut wraps (5)
- Eggs (2 beaten with 1 tsp. water)
- Coconut oil (4 T + .5 c divided)

- Frozen spinach (10 oz. thawed, dried)
- Pine nuts (.25 c)
- Garlic (2 cloves)
- Parmesan cheese (1 oz.)
- Basil leaves (2 c)
- Balsamic vinegar (as desired)
- Mixed salad greens (5 oz.)

What to Do
- Ensure your oven is heated to 350 degrees F.
- Add the coconut oil to a skillet before placing it on the stove over a burner turned to a medium heat. Add in the spinach and let it cook 2 minutes before removing it and placing it in a mixing bowl.
- Add the .25 c parmesan cheese and the mascarpone to the bowl and mix well to combine thoroughly.
- Line up 50 percent of the wraps on a cutting board before brushing them using the water and egg mixture. Place 1 T of the spinach mixture into each corner of each wrap, leaving as much space as possible between the scoops.
- Brush one of the remaining wraps with the egg mixture and then use it to cover the tops of the filled wraps. Press down on the edges to create pockets and then use a ravioli cutter to cut out four squares total.
- Add the remaining ingredients to a blender and blend well to create the pesto.
- Place the rest of the coconut oil into a pan before placing the pan on the stove over a burner turned to a medium heat. Add the ravioli to the pan in batches, each should take about 2 minutes to cook, flip them at the 1 minute mark.

Enchiladas

Total Prep & Cooking Time: 45 minutes
Yields: 8 Servings

What to Use
- Black pepper (as desired)
- Sea salt (as desired)
- Raw honey (1 tsp.)
- Paprika (.25 tsp.)
- Coconut aminos (1 tsp.)
- Oregano (.5 tsp. dried)
- Flour tortillas (8 warmed)
- Bone broth (2 c divided)
- Chicken (8 oz. shredded)
- Goat cheese (8 oz. crumbled)
- Cumin (.5 tsp. ground)
- Apple cider vinegar (3 tsp.)
- Garlic (4 cloves peeled)
- Shiitake mushrooms (8 oz. chopped)
- Olive oil (2 T)

What to Do
- Ensure your oven is heated to 400 degrees F.
- Add the oil to a skillet before placing it on the stove over a burner turned to a medium/high heat. Add in the mushrooms and onions and allow them to cook about 6 minutes, stirring regularly.
- Mix in the pepper, salt and .5 c broth before reducing the heat to medium and letting everything cook about 4 minutes.
- Once all the broth has been absorbed you will want to place all of the ingredients into a mixing bowl before stirring in half of the goat cheese.

- Add the rest of the broth, paprika, oregano, honey, cumin, 2 tsp. sea salt, coconut aminos, garlic, apple cider vinegar and the rest of the broth in a blender and pulse until smooth. Add .5 c of the sauce to a glass dish (9 x 13).
- Add .25 c of the mushroom mixture to each tortilla before folding up the bottom and then rolling it tightly. Place the finished tortillas into the baking dish and cover them with the sauce. Top all of the tortillas with the rest of the sauce and the remaining cheese.
- Place the baking dish in the oven for about 15 minutes. You will know they are ready when the cheese is melted and the sauce is bubbling.

Baked Sweet Potato

Total Prep & Cooking Time: 20 minutes
Yields: 2 Servings

What to Use
- Black pepper (as desired)
- Sea salt (as desired)
- Garlic (.25 tsp.)
- Kale (.5 c)
- Olive oil (.25 tsp.)
- Sweet potato (6 oz.)

What to Do
- Ensure your oven is heated to 350 degrees F.
- Add the sweet potatoes to pieces of aluminum foil, taking care to pierce the potato in numerous places to allow for venting. Coat the potatoes in the foil and then place them on a baking sheet.
- Place the baking sheet in the oven and let them cook for 30 minutes, you will know they are ready wen they are soft all the way through.
- Once they are finished cooking, remove the potatoes from the foil and place them in a large bowl. Mash the potatoes with the salt, pepper, garlic, olive oil and kale.

Bok Choy And Fried Shrimp

Total Prep & Cooking Time: 10 minutes
Yields: 4 Servings

What to Use
- Bok choy (.75 c)
- Garlic (.5 tsp.)
- Ginger (.25 tsp.)
- Sesame oil (.25 tsp.)
- Wild shrimp (24 oz.)

What to Do
- Add all of the ingredients to a wok and stir fry for 10 minutes.
- Serve hot.

Fettuccine

Total Prep & Cooking Time: 30 minutes
Yields: 4 Servings

What to Use
- Black pepper (as desired)
- Sea salt (as desired)
- Mascarpone (1 c)
- Asparagus (1 bunch chopped)
- Parmesan cheese (.25 c grated)
- Shitake mushrooms (5 oz. sliced)
- Shirataki fettuccine noodles (32 oz. cooked)
- Extra-virgin olive oil (.25 c)
- Italian parsley (.5 c)
- Italian seasoning (.5 tsp.)

What to Do
- Cook the pasta according to the provided instructions and keep 1 c of the water used to cook the noodles.
- Add the oil to a skillet before placing it on the stove over a burner turned to a medium heat. Add in the mushrooms and increase the heat to high/medium and cook for 2 minutes before adding in the asparagus, the remaining oil and .5 tsp. salt. Cook until the asparagus is tender and crisp which should be about 3 minutes.
- Turn off the heat before adding in the mascarpone and shirataki noodles before tossing to coat. Add .25 c of the reserved noodle water at a time to thin the sauce and keep the noodles moist. Stir in the remaining ingredients and serve warm.

Meatballs And Salad

Total Prep & Cooking Time: 45 minutes
Yields: 6 Servings

What to Use
- Black pepper (as desired)
- Sea salt (as desired)
- Raw honey (2 tsp.)
- Coconut aminos (1 T)
- Sesame coconut oil (1 T)
- Red pepper (.5 tsp.)
- Lime juice (3 T)
- Scallions (4 sliced thin)
- Cilantro (.5 c)
- Shitake mushrooms (.5 c sautéed)
- Meatballs (12 cooked)
- Baby bok choy (6 heads)
- Coconut oil (2 T)

What to Do
- Add the coconut oil to a skillet before placing it on the stove over a burner turned to a medium heat. Add in the mushrooms and allow them to cook about 5 minutes. Add in the meatballs and let everything cook until they are warm.

- In a serving bowl, add the honey, coconut aminos, sesame oil, red pepper and lime juice and mix well. Add in the scallions, cilantro, bok choy and the mixture from the skillet and toss to coat.

Coconut Chicken

Total Prep & Cooking Time: 30 minutes
Yields: 4 Servings

What to Use
- Black pepper (as desired)
- Sea salt (as desired)
- Coconut milk (1 c)
- 5 spice powder (1 tsp.)
- Kosher salt (1 tsp.)
- Coconut aminos (3 T)
- Drumsticks (10 skin removed)
- Onion (1 sliced thin, peeled)
- Fish sauce (2 T)
- Ginger (1 in. peeled, chopped)
- Cilantro (.25 c)
- Garlic (4 cloves crushed, peeled)
- Lime juice (1 lime)
- Lemongrass (1 stalk chopped, skinned)
- Coconut oil (1 tsp.)

What to Do
- Add the ginger, fish sauce, garlic, lemongrass, coconut aminos and 5 spice powder in a blender before adding in the coconut milk and using the pulse setting to blend.
- Add the drumsticks to a bowl and season as desired before adding in the blender mixture and ensuring the drumsticks are well-coated.
- Turn on your Instant Pot and set it to the sauté setting and allow it to heat up before adding in the sliced onions and coconut oil and letting them cook about 5 minutes.
- Add the drumsticks and the marinade to the Instant Pot and select the warm option before sealing and locking the lid.

- Select the Manual option and then set the timer for 15 minutes and high pressure.
- Use the manual release valve when the drumsticks are done.
- Season with fish sauce prior to serving.

Arugula Salad With Sweet Potato

Total Prep & Cooking Time: 20 minutes
Yields: 4 Servings

What to Use
- Black pepper (as desired)
- Sea salt (as desired)
- Parmesan cheese (.25 c)
- Baby arugula (5 oz.)
- Dijon mustard (1 T)
- White wine vinegar (1 T)
- Swiss cheese (2 oz. shredded)
- Prosciutto (2 oz.)
- Sweet potat0 (1 lb. cubed, peeled)
- Coconut oil (.25 c)
- Tarragon leaves (.25 c chopped)

What to Do
- Add your sweet potatoes to a boiler and then cover them with water. Allow them to boil before adding some salt and then reducing the temperature to let them simmer about 12 minutes. After they are done cooking drain them, run cold water oven them and then deposit them on a cutting board and dice them.
- In a small bowl, combine the pepper, mustard, salt, oil and vinegar and mix well.
- Split the arugula between 4 bowls before adding in the tarragon, sweet potatoes, prosciutto and swiss cheese. Top with dressing and parmesan prior to serving.

Chicken And Cabbage With Apples And Cranberries

Total Prep & Cooking Time: 35 minutes
Yields: 4 Servings

What to Use
- Black pepper (as desired)
- Sea salt (as desired)
- Apple cider vinegar (1 T)
- Ginger (1 tsp. ground)
- Chicken bone broth (.5 c)
- Apples (2 sliced)
- Chicken breast (2 lbs. boneless, skinless)
- Cranberries (1 c frozen)
- Raw honey (1 T)
- Cabbage (1 head cored)
- Cinnamon (1 tsp.)

What to Do
- Add all of the ingredients to your Instant Pot and select the poultry setting prior to closing and securing the lid. Set the timer for 20 minutes.
- Allow the pressure to release naturally for 10 minutes.
- Serve hot and enjoy!

Mushroom Mini Pizza

Total Prep & Cooking Time: 35 minutes
Yields: 2 Servings

What to Use
- Black pepper (as desired)
- Sea salt (as desired)
- Prosciutto (2 slices)
- Buffalo mozzarella (1 ball sliced)
- Basil pesto (6 T)
- Coconut oil (2 T)
- Portobello mushrooms (2 caps)

What to Do
- Ensure your oven is heated to 325 degrees F.
- Add the mushrooms caps to a baking pan before coating them in coconut oil. Place them in the oven for 5 minutes before removing the baking sheet from the oven, flipping the mushroom caps and returning them to the oven for an additional 5 minutes. The end result should be both crispy and brown on top.
- Add 3 T pesto to each cap, top with a slice of prosciutto and then the mozzarella.
- Return the mushrooms to the baking sheet and return the sheet to the oven for an additional 5 minutes.
- Season prior to serving hot.

Orange Salmon Salad

Total Prep & Cooking Time: 30 minutes
Yields: 4 Servings

What to Use
- Black pepper (as desired)
- Sea salt (as desired)
- Dijon mustard (1 tsp.)
- Coconut oil (4 T)
- White wine vinegar (3 T)
- Raw honey (1 tsp.)
- Dill (1 T chopped)
- Lemon juice (1 lemon)
- Navel oranges (2 sectioned, peeled)
- Red onion (1 sliced thin)
- Salmon (1 lb. broiled, flaked)
- Baby spinach (5 oz.)
- Feta cheese (2 oz. crumbled)
- Hazelnuts (.3 c chopped, toasted)

What to Do

- In a serving bowl, combine the flaked salmon, navel orange pieces, spinach and red onions.
- In a separate bowl, add the feta cheese and hazelnuts and toss to combine before combining the two bowls and mixing well.
- In a small bowl, mix together the Dijon mustard, coconut oil, white wine vinegar, honey, dill and lemon juice and whisk well.
- Add the dressing to the salad and toss to coat.

Chapter 5: Dinner Recipes

Spinach Salad With Steak

Total Prep & Cooking Time: 25 minutes
Yields: 4 Servings

What to Use
- Black pepper (as desired)
- Sea salt (as desired)
- Red wine vinegar (2 T)
- Thyme (2 tsp. dried)
- Goat milk yogurt (4 oz.)
- Shirataki rice (1 c rinsed, drained)
- Baby spinach (5 oz.)
- Grass-fed steak (1 lb.)
- Pine nuts (2 T)

What to Do
- Add the steak to a skillet before placing it on the stove over a burner turned to a medium heat. Prepare your steak to its desired level of doneness.
- While the steak is cooking, add the pepper, salt, thyme, yogurt and red wine vinegar in a small bowl and whisk well.
- Cook the rice according to instructions.
- Plate the spinach in four separate bowls before topping with sliced steak, pine nuts, rice and dressing.

Noodles With Broccoli And Pesto

Total Prep & Cooking Time: 20 minutes
Yields: 4 Servings

What to Use
- Black pepper (as desired)
- Sea salt (as desired)
- Broccoli florets (1 c)
- Olive oil (.25 tsp.)
- Basil pesto (.5 c)
- Miracle noodles (1 bag cooked)

What to Do
- Add the coconut oil to a skillet before placing it on the stove over a burner turned to a medium heat. Add in the broccoli florets, pesto and noodles and let everything cook about 10 minutes, mixing regularly.
- Season as desired prior to serving.

Squash Soup

Total Prep & Cooking Time: 45 minutes
Yields: 4 Servings

What to Use
- Black pepper (as desired)
- Sea salt (as desired)
- Thyme (2 T)
- Chives (2 T)
- Coconut milk (1 can)
- Oregano (2 T)
- Chicken stock (6 c)
- Garlic (4 cloves peeled)
- Celery (2 c)
- Salt (1.5 T)
- Herbs de Provence 93 T)
- Carrots (3)
- Cayenne pepper (.25 T)
- Onion (1 sliced)
- Butternut squash (1 peeled)
- Parsley leaves (.25 c)

What to Do
- Slice the butternut squash in half before trimming off the ends and removing the seeds. Dice the remaining squash.
- Add all of the ingredients, except the coconut milk to your pressure cooker, saving the chicken stock and seasonings for last.
- Secure the lid of the pressure cooker and choose the soup option. Allow the Instant Pot to cook for 30 minutes and then release the pressure manually.
- Pour the results into an immersion blender and blend your soup until smooth.

- Add in the coconut milk and season as desired.
- Serve hot.

Sweet Potato Gnocchi

Total Prep & Cooking Time: 60 minutes
Yields: 4 Servings

What to Use
- Black pepper (as desired)
- Sea salt (as desired)
- Parmesan cheese (.25 c)
- Lemon (1 zested, juiced)
- Garlic (1 clove crushed)
- Coconut oil (3 T)
- Basil (.5 c torn, divided)
- Sweet potato (peeled, chunked)
- Egg (1)
- Sea salt (.5 tsp.)
- Cassava flour (.5 c)

What to Do
- Place the sweet potatoes in a pot before filling the pot with water so the gnocchi is covered in about 2 inches of water before placing the pot on the stove over a burner turned to a high heat. Bring the pot to a boil before turning down the heat and allowing the pot to simmer for 15 minutes partially covered. Drain the potatoes, rinse them with cold water, and then drain.
- Place the sweet potatoes in a bowl and mash them before adding in the egg and a pinch of salt. Add in the flour and the knead the mixture until it forms a dough. If the dough sticks to your fingers add more flour.
- Add a pinch of salt to a pot of water before placing the pot on the stove over a burner turned to a high heat.

- While waiting for the water to boil roll the dough into long, think rolls about the width of a thumb. Chop each roll into 1-inch pieces and put a shallow indent in each.
- Place the gnocchi in the water using a slotted spoon. When they start to float they are ready to be removed. Place the finished gnocchi in a covered bowl to keep them warm.
- Add the oil to the skillet before placing it on the stove over a burner turned to a medium heat. Add in the garlic and let it cook about 4 minutes before adding the gnocchi and basil to the skillet and mix well. Cook about 2 minutes before adding in the pepper, lemon zest, lemon juice and salt.
- Top with cheese and basil prior to serving.

Chili

Total Prep & Cooking Time: 6 hours and 15 minutes
Yields: 8 Servings

What to Use
- Black pepper (as desired)
- Sea salt (as desired)
- Sweet potato puree (15 oz.)
- Red wine vinegar (2 tsp.)
- Chili powder (2 T)
- Celery (3 ribs diced fine)
- Onion (1 diced)
- Beef bone broth (2 c)
- Cloves (1 pinch ground)
- Cinnamon (1 pinch ground)
- Adobo sauce (1 T)
- Cumin (2 tsp. ground)
- Garlic (4 cloves minced)
- Grass-feed beef (2 lbs. ground)
- Avocado oil (1 T divided)
- Coconut aminos (2 tsp.)

What to Do

- Add the coconut oil to a skillet before placing it on the stove over a burner turned to a high heat. Add in .5 tsp. salt along with the ground beef and allow the meat to brown, using a spatula to break it up as you go. After about 5 minutes place the meat in your slow cooker.
- Reduce the burner heat to medium before adding in another tsp. of oil along with the onion, celery and garlic. Let everything cook for 5 minutes before adding in the chili powder, cinnamon, cloves and cumin. Let everything cook an additional 60 seconds while you stir. Add in the bone broth and let everything cook an additional 30 seconds before adding the contents of the skillet to the slow cooker.
- Add in the coconut aminos, vinegar, adobo sauce, sweet potato puree and season as desired.
- Cover the slow cooker and allow it to cook on a low heat for 6 hours.
- Top with lime wedges, scallions and sour cream prior to serving.

Instant Pot Chicken

Total Prep & Cooking Time: 50 minutes
Yields: 4 Servings

What to Use
- Black pepper (as desired)
- Sea salt (as desired)
- Cilantro (.25 c)
- Ginger (1 in. chopped fine)
- Apple cider vinegar (2 T divided)
- Coconut aminos (.25 c + 1 T)
- Lime juice (1 lime)
- Garlic cloves (4)
- Salt (.5 tsp.)
- Raw honey (2 T)
- Mango (1 chunks)
- Green onion (1 sliced)
- Red onion (.5 chopped)
- Fish sauce (1 tsp)
- Chicken bone broth (.5 c)
- Chicken thighs (8 deboned)
- Cooking fat (1 T)

What to Do
- Heat your Instant Pot by pressing the sauté button before adding in the fat and allowing it to melt.
- Add in the chicken thighs with the skin facing down and allow it to cook for 3 minutes before flipping and allowing it to cook for 2 minutes more.
- Remove the chicken from the Instant Pot before adding in the garlic, mango and onion and allow them to cook about 5 minutes.

- Cancel the Instant Pot's sauté option before adding in the chicken, 1 T apple cider vinegar, honey, fish sauce, coconut aminos, chicken bone broth, lime juice, cilantro and ginger and mix well.
- Put the lid on the Instant Pot and select the poultry setting before choosing the option for high pressure which will automatically set a timer for 15 minutes.
- Manually release the pressure fully before removing the lid and removing the chicken from the Instant Pot.
- Add in the remaining apple cider vinegar and coconut aminos, along with a pinch of salt and return the Instant Pot to the sauté setting to allow the sauce to reduce until it reaches your desired level of thickness.
- Plate chicken and top with sauce and green onion prior to serving.

Cream Soup

Total Prep & Cooking Time: 20 minutes
Yields: 4 Servings

What to Use
- Black pepper (as desired)
- Sea salt (as desired)
- Broccoli (2 c florets)
- Garlic (2 cloves chopped, peeled)
- Coconut milk (500 mL)
- Coconut flour (.25 c)
- Bay leaf (1)
- Rutabaga (2 c)
- Basil (.5 tsp. dried)
- Raw honey (1 tsp.)
- White onion (1 c diced)
- Beef bone broth (2 c)
- Grass-fed beef (1 lb.)
- Plantain (2 c)
- Cinnamon (.5 tsp.)
- Water (6 c)
- Carrots (1 c)

What to Do
- Add the water to your Instant Pot and use the sauté option to bring it to a boil before adding in your meat and letting it cook about 3 minutes.
- Drain the water and return the meat to the pot before adding in the bone broth as well as the vegetables before seasoning it with the cinnamon, herbs, salt and pepper and mixing well.
- Cover and seal the Instant Pot before setting it to 20 minutes.

- Use the quick release valve when time has elapsed and remove the vegetables and meat when it is safe to do so.
- Return the Instant Pot to the sauté setting before adding in the honey, coconut flour and coconut milk and mix well.
- Add in the broccoli and allow it to simmer before removing the cinnamon and bay leaf once the broccoli has finished cooking.
- Add all of the ingredients to a blender and blend well
- Season prior to serving.

Taco Cups

Total Prep & Cooking Time: 90 minutes
Yields: 12 Servings

What to Use
- Black pepper (as desired)
- Sea salt (as desired)
- Chili powder (2 tsp.)
- Black beans (2 cans)
- Garlic powder (.25 tsp.)
- Onion (1 chopped fine)
- Avocado oil (3 T)
- Paprika (.5 tsp.)
- Coriander (1 tsp.)
- Palm shortening (.25 c)
- Coconut milk (.5 c room temp.)
- Cassava flour (1 c)
- Coconut aminos (1 tsp)
- Oregano (.5 tsp. dried)
- Water (.25 c)
- Taco cups (12)
- Ground cumin (2 tsp.)

What to Do
- Ensure your oven is heated to 425 degrees F.
- Prepare a muffin pan by turning it upside down and greasing it using 1 T avocado oil.
- In a mixing bowl, combine the water, palm shortening, cassava flour and coconut milk together and blend well.
- Form the resulting dough into 12 single oz. balls before rolling each ball out flat and placing them between 2 pieces of parchment paper

- Add the coconut oil to a skillet before placing it on the stove over a burner turned to a medium heat.
- Place the pieces of dough over the underside of the muffin cups to create bowls. Place the muffin tin in the oven for 20 minutes.
- Let the cups cool prior to filling.
- While the cups are baking, add the remaining oil to a skilling before placing it on top of a burner turned a medium heat. Add in the onions and let them cook for 2 minutes, stirring constantly. Add in the spice and coconut aminos and ensure the onions are well-coated before letting them cook an additional 60 seconds while stirring.
- Add the onions and black beans to the Instant Pot and season as desired. Close and seal the Instant Pot and turn it to a high pressure and cook 5 minutes. Let the pressure release naturally before seasoning as desired.
- Fill taco cups prior to serving.

Stuffed Peppers

Total Prep & Cooking Time: 6 hours and 10 minutes
Yields: 5 Servings

What to Use
- Thyme (2 tsp. dried)
- Oregano (2 tsp. dried)
- Basil (2 tsp. dried)
- Garlic (.5 clove minced)
- White onion (1 small, diced)
- Cauliflower (.5 head processed to resemble rice)
- Bell peppers (5 seeded, peeled)
- Italian hot sausage (1 lb.)

What to Do
- Start by removing the top part of each pepper from the rest of the pepper. Save the top part of each pepper but remove and discard the seeds.
- Add the processed cauliflower to a mixing bowl before mixing in the onion, garlic, basil, thyme and oregano and combining well.

- Add the sausage to a skillet and place the skillet on the stove over a burner turned to a high/medium heat until it sears just enough to add to the favor.
- Add the sausage to the bowl of cauliflower and mix well.
- Add the results to the hollowed out peppers before placing each into your slow cooker and adding the tops of the peppers back in as well.
- Cover the slow cooker and let it cook on a low heat for 6 hours.
- Serve hot and enjoy.

Curry With Pineapple

Total Prep & Cooking Time: 6 hours and 5 minutes
Yields: 6 Servings

What to Use
- Black pepper (to taste)
- Salt (to taste)
- Lime juice (1 lime)
- Sweet potatoes (3 cups cubed)
- Carrot (3 chopped)
- Garlic (1 clove minced)
- Onion (.5 large diced)
- Garam masala (2 tsp.)
- Turmeric powder (.25 tsp.)
- Curry powder (.5 T)
- Vegetable stock (1 cup)
- Pumpkin puree (2 cups)
- Coconut milk (15 oz. unsweetened, full fat)

What to Do
- Add the pepper, salt, Garam masala, turmeric powder, curry powder, vegetable stock, pumpkin puree and coconut milk to the slow cooker before mixing well.
- Mix in the lime juice, sweet potatoes, carrots, garlic and onion and stir well.
- Cover the slow cooker and let it cook on a low heat for 6 hours.
- Serve hot over rice and enjoy.

Flap Steak

Total Prep & Cooking Time: 4 hours and 30 minutes
Yields: 4 Servings

What to Use
- Black pepper (as needed)
- Salt (as needed)
- Coconut oil (2 T)
- Mango Salsa (as needed)
- Cumin (.5 tsp.)
- Coriander (.5 tsp.)
- Lime juice (1 T)
- White onion (.25 minced)
- Olive oil (.5 cups)
- Parsley (1 cup packed)
- Cilantro (1 cup packed)
- Flap steak (2 lbs. sliced thin)

What to Do
- In a food processor, combine .5 tsp. salt, cumin, coriander, lime juice, white onion, olive oil, parsley and cilantro and process well.
- Add the steak and half of the contents of a food processor to a resalable plastic bag before placing in the refrigerator to marinate for 4 hours.
- Let the steak sit at room temperature for half an hour before heating your grill to a high heat and cooking the meat for approximately 2 minutes on each side.
- Top with the remaining marinade prior to serving.

Chowder

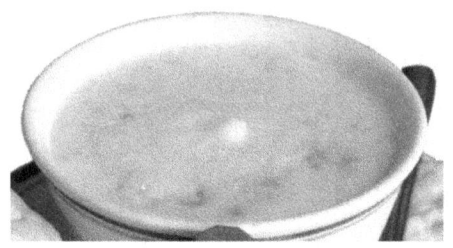

Total Prep & Cooking Time: 55 minutes
Yields: 5 Servings

What to Use
- Black pepper (as needed)
- Salt (as needed)
- Parsley (.25 cups chopped rough)
- Bay leaves (2)
- Chicken broth (6 cups)
- Thyme (1 tsp. dried)
- Oregano (1 tsp. dried)
- Smoked paprika (1 tsp.)
- Garlic powder (1 tsp.)
- Garlic (2 cloves chopped)
- Yellow onion (1 chopped)
- Celery (4 stalks diced)
- Carrots (2 diced, peeled)
- Shrimp (1 lb. deveined, peeled)
- Bacon (1.5 lbs.)
- Cauliflower (1 head florets, steamed, pureed)

What to Do

- Place a Dutch oven on the stove on top of a burner turned to a medium heat. Add in the bacon and let it cook until it reaches the desired level of crispness. Remove the bacon from the oven and add in the shrimp before seasoning as needed and cooking each side for 2 minutes.
- Add in the garlic, onion, celery and carrots and toss them in the bacon fat. After you can begin to see through the onion, mix in the salt, thyme, oregano, smoked paprika and garlic powder and stir for 60 seconds.
- Mix in the bay leaves as well as the chicken broth and the cauliflower. Mix in half of the cooked bacon and let it cook for 15 minutes.
- Take the bay leaves out of the mixture before adding in the parsley and pureeing everything in the Dutch Oven.
- Add in the shrimp and heat completely.
- Garnish with parsley, olive oil and bacon prior to serving.

Pot Roast

Total Prep & Cooking Time: 7 hours and 10 minutes
Yields: 6 Servings

What to Use-The Roast
- Parsley (1 T chopped)
- Garlic (3 cloves chopped)
- Onion (.5 sliced)
- Celery (2 stalks diced)
- Carrots (5 diced, peeled)
- Beef stock (1 cup)
- Coconut oil (1 T)
- Beef roast (3 lbs. fat removed)
- Allspice (.5 tsp. ground)
- Clove (.5 tsp. ground)
- Salt (1.5 tsp. ground)
- Cinnamon (2 tsp.)
- Coriander (1 T ground)
- Pepper (1 T)

What to Do
- Combine the allspice, clove, salt, cinnamon, coriander and pepper together and spread it over the meat.
- Place a skillet on the stove over a burner with the heat turned to medium before adding the coconut oil.
- Place the roast in the skillet and sear each side for a total of 10 minutes.
- Place the roast in the slow cooker along with the celery, garlic, onion and carrots.
- Add in the broth and let the slow cooker cook at a low temperature for 7 hours.
- Add the parsley on top, serve and enjoy.

Salmon With Capers

Total Prep & Cooking Time: 30 minutes
Yields: 4 Servings

What to Use
- Olive oil (to taste)
- Salt (to taste)
- Pepper (to taste)
- Thyme (1 T crushed)
- Capers (1 T)
- Lemon (1 thinly sliced)
- Salmon (32 oz.)

What to Do
- Cover a baking sheet with a rim in parchment paper.
- Put the salmon onto the baking sheet so that its skin touches the baking sheet.
- Add salt and pepper to the fish as you prefer before topping the fish with the caper, thyme and lemon.
- Place the fish in a cold oven, set the oven at 400 degrees Fahrenheit and let the fish cook for 25 minutes.
- Serve hot and enjoy.

Squash And Thai Curry

Total Prep & Cooking Time: 30 minutes
Yields: 4 Servings

What to Use
- Cauliflower rice (preparation details described below)
- Cilantro (.25 cups chopped)
- Lime juice (2 tsp.)
- Acorn Squash (1 peeled, seeded and cubed)
- Coconut aminos (1 T)
- Coconut milk (14 oz. can)
- Red curry paste (3 T)
- Ginger (1-inch peeled, minced)
- Garlic (4 cloves minced)
- Bell pepper (1 sliced)
- Salt (1 T)
- Onion (1 diced)
- Coconut oil (1 T)

What to Do
- Place a large pan on a burner which has been turned to a medium heat.
- Add in the coconut oil and the onion and let it cook for 6 minutes, be sure to stir.
- Mix in the salt, ginger, garlic and bell pepper and let cook for 60 seconds.
- Mix in the curry paste and let cook for an additional 60 seconds.
- Mix in the coconut aminos and milk before bringing the pan to a simmer.
- Mix in the squash and let the pan simmer for 20 minutes or until the squash has begun to grow tender.
- Take the pan from the heat, mix in the lime juice.

- Serve with cauliflower rice.

Chicken And Blackberry Mustard

Total Prep & Cooking Time: 20 minutes
Yields: 4 Servings

What to Use
- Blackberries (1 cup chopped)
- Mustard (1.5 T)
- Honey (2 tsp.)
- Chicken tenders (1 lb. halved)
- Salt (.5 tsp.)
- Black pepper (.25 tsp.)
- Cornmeal (3 T)
- Coconut oil (3 T)

What to Do
- Season the chicken as desired before adding it to a bowl of the cornmeal and coating well.
- Add the coconut oil to the skillet before adding the skillet to a burner turned to a high/medium heat.
- After the oil has melted, lower the heat to medium and add in the chicken and let each side cook for about 4 minutes. The internal temperature should read 165 degrees Fahrenheit.
- Remove the tenders from the stove and let them cool for a few minutes prior to serving.
- Add the mustard, honey and berries together, max and mix well.
- Serve with the chicken and enjoy.

Fish Sandwich

Total Prep & Cooking Time: 20 minutes
Yields: 4 Servings

What to Use
- Salmon fillet (1 lb. quartered)
- Cajun seasoning (2 tsp.)
- Avocado (1 pitted, peeled)
- Mayonnaise (2 T)
- White rolls (4)
- Arugula (1 cup)
- Red onion (.5 cups sliced thin)
- Coconut oil (2 T)

What to Do
- Coat the grill in coconut oil before ensuring it is heated to a high heat.
- Coat the fish using the seasoning before adding it to the grill and let it cook for approximately 3 minutes on each side.
- Mash the avocado before mixing it with the mayonnaise and spreading on the rolls prior to serving.
- Season as required, serve hot and enjoy.

Chicken Pesto

Total Prep & Cooking Time: 45 minutes
Yields: 4 Servings

What to Use
- Black pepper (as desired)
- Sea salt (as desired)
- Olive oil (4 T)
- Leafy greens (5.3 oz.)
- Garlic (1 clove chopped fine)
- Feta cheese (8 oz. diced)
- Olives (8 T pitted)
- Heavy whipping cream (1.5 c)
- Green pesto (3 oz.)
- Butter (2 oz.)
- Chicken thighs (1.5 lbs.)

What to do
- Ensure your oven is heated to 400F.
- Cut the chicken into pieces before seasoning as desired and frying until it reaches an internal temperature of 165F.
- In a small mixing bowl, combine the heavy cream and the pesto.
- Add the chicken to a baking dish before adding in the garlic, feta cheese and olives and topping everything with the pesto mixture.
- Place the dish in the oven and let it cook for 30 minutes.

Meat Pie

Total Prep & Cooking Time: 15 minutes
Yields: 4 Servings

What to Use-Filling
- Water (.5 c)
- Dried oregano (1 T)
- Sea salt (as desired)
- Black pepper (as desired)
- Ground lamb (1.3 lbs.)
- Olive oil (2 T)
- Garlic (1 clove chopped fine)
- Yellow onion (.5 chopped fine)

What to Use-Crust
- Water (4 T)
- Egg (1 large, organic)
- Coconut oil (3 T)
- Salt (1 pinch)
- Baking powder (1 tsp.)
- Psyllium husk powder (1 T)
- Coconut powder (4 T)
- Almond flour (.75 c)

What to Use-Toppings
- Shredded cheese (7 oz.)
- Cottage cheese (8 oz.)

What to do
- Ensure your oven is heated to 350F.
- Add the olive oil to a skillet before placing it on the stove over a burned turned to a high/medium heat. Add in the

- garlic along with the onion and let them fry for 3 minutes or until they have softened.
- Add in the ground beef, basil and oregano and season as desired before adding in the tomato paste as well as the water. Reduce the heat and let everything simmer 20 minutes. While this is taking place, make the crust.
- Combine the dough ingredients using a food processor and process until the results form a ball. The same effect can be achieved by hand mixing with a fork.
- Line greased 10-inch springform pan before spreading in the dough.
- Bake the crust for 15 minutes before removing it and adding in the filling.
- Mix together the shredded cheese and cottage cheese and add this on top.
- Bake 30 minutes and let sit 5 minutes prior to baking.

Turkey Wings

Total Prep & Cooking Time: 30 minutes
Yields: 4 Servings

What to Use
- Chopped thyme (1 bunch)
- Orange juice (1 c.)
- Chopped yellow onion (1)
- Pepper
- Salt
- Walnuts (1 c.)
- Dried cranberries (1.5 c.)
- Olive oil (2 Tbsp.)
- Coconut oil (2 T melted)
- Turkey wings (4)

What to Do
- Set your Instant Pot on Sauté mode and add the oil and ghee. When these are warm, add the pepper, salt, and turkey wings. Let the wings heat up on all sides.
- Add the thyme, cranberries, walnuts, and onion. Stir these around and cook for two minutes.
- Add the orange juice and then cover up the pot. Cook these on High for 20 minutes.
- Divide up the wings between a few plates and keep them warm.
- Set the pot to Simmer mode and cook your cranberry mix for another 5 minutes. Drizzle this on the turkey wings and serve.

Butternut And Chard Soup

Total Prep & Cooking Time: 30 minutes
Yields: 6 Servings

What to Use
- Coconut cream (1 c.)
- Minced garlic cloves (4)
- Cubed butternut squash (2 c.)
- Hopped Swiss chard (4 c.)
- Chopped rosemary (1 tsp.)
- Pepper
- Salt
- Chicken stock (8 c.)
- Thyme sprigs (4)
- Chopped celery stalks (3)
- Chopped carrots (3)
- Chopped yellow onion (1)
- Olive oil (1 Tbsp.)

What to Do
- Set the Instant Pot to Sauté mode before adding the oil. Add the celery, onion, and carrots.
- After those are warm, add the rosemary, garlic, butternut squash, pepper, salt, chicken stock, and thyme. Stir and cook this on a high setting for 18 minutes.
- Discard the thyme and add the coconut cream and Swiss chard. Warm up before serving.

Garlic Pot Roast

Total Prep & Cooking Time: 5 hours and 10 minutes
Yields: 8 Servings

What to Use
- Salt (as needed)
- Pepper (as needed)
- Beef stock (.75 cups)
- Garlic (1 tsp. minced0
- Bacon (6 slices, crumbled cooked)
- Beef shoulder (3 lbs.)

What to do
- Add the roast to the slow cooker and season as desired before topping with bacon and minced garlic.
- Add in the beef stock and set the slow cooker, covered, to high and let everything sit for 5 hours until the meat has reached its desired level of tenderness.

Meatballs

Total Prep & Cooking Time: 40 minutes
Yields: 3 Servings

What to Use
- Coconut oil (2 T)
- Pepper (as desired)
- Salt (as desired)
- Oregano (1 T)
- White onion (2 T diced)
- Garlic (2 T minced)
- Bacon (9 slices)
- Italian sausage (1 lb.)

What to Do
- Start by making sure your oven is heated to 375F.
- Cover a baking sheet using aluminum foil.
- Place a skillet on top of a burner that has been turned to a high/medium heat before adding in the coconut oil and the sausage and letting it brown.
- Add all of the ingredients, save the bacon to a mixing bowl and combine thoroughly.
- Form the results into 9 meatballs and wrap a slice of bacon around each before placing them on the baking sheet. Place the baking sheet in the oven for 30 minutes or until the bacon is well-cooked.
- Let cool 5 minutes prior to serving.

Sliders

Total Prep & Cooking Time: 45 minutes
Yields: 6 Servings

What to Use
- Water (.25 c)
- Heavy cream (.25 c)
- Salt (.5 tsp.)
- Garlic powder (.5 tsp.)
- Cheddar cheese (4 oz.)
- Butter (2 oz. unsalted)
- Carbquik (2 c)
- Hamburger (1 lb.)
- Cheddar cheese (6 slices)

What to Do
- Start by making sure your oven is heated to 450F.
- In a mixing bowl, add in the Carbquick before adding in the butter and mixing until the results start to form a dough.
- Add in the garlic powder, cheese and salt and mix well before adding in the liquid ingredients and mixing to form a dough.
- Form the dough into 6 equal sections and place them onto a prepared baking sheet.
- Place the baking sheet in the oven for 8 minutes until the biscuits are golden brown.
- While the biscuits are baking, place the hamburger into a skillet and place the skillet on top of a burner turned to a high/medium heat. As the meat browns, form it into small patties.
- Slice the biscuits in half, and a hamburger patty and slice of cheese to each.

Burger With Egg

Total Prep & Cooking Time: 30 minutes
Yields: 3 Servings

What to Use
- Cheddar cheese (8 oz.)
- Worcestershire sauce (to taste)
- Onion powder (.5 tsp.)
- Garlic powder (.5 tsp.)
- Egg (2)
- Ground beef (1.5 lbs.)
- Coconut oil (2 T)
- Bacon (4 strips)

What to Do
- In a mixing bowl, combine the eggs and beef and mix well before adding in the spices and combining thoroughly.
- Break the results down into 1.5 oz. patties before topping each patty with .5 oz. of cheese.
- Combine every 2 patties into a single burger.
- Add the coconut oil to a pan before placing the pan on the stove on top of a burner turned to a high/medium heat. Add in one of the patties and cook each side for approximately 2 minutes or until it reaches your desired level of doneness.
- In a separate frying pan, add in the bacon before placing it on top of a burner turned to a high/medium heat and cook until crispy.
- Top each patty with bacon prior to serving.

Chapter 6: Snack Recipes

Stuffed Poblano Peppers

Total Prep & Cooking Time: 4 hours and 5 minutes
Yields: 4 Servings

What to Use
- Salt (as needed)
- Pepper (as needed)
- Onion (1 T chopped)
- Ground beef (.3 lbs.)
- Cauliflower (.3 c chopped fine)
- Poblano pepper (1)

What to Do
- Slice the poblano pepper in two and remove all of the seeds before setting it aside.
- Place the onion and the ground beef in a skillet before placing the skillet on the stove over a burner turned to a high/medium heat and cook for approximately 5 minutes. Stir regularly to ensure the ground beef browns fully.
- Add the results to the poblano halves.
- Add the tomato juice to the slow cooker before placing the stuffed peppers on top.
- Adjust the slow cooker temperature to low and leave it be, covered for about 4 hours.

Hummus

Total Prep & Cooking Time: 120 minutes
Yields: 18 Servings

What to Use
- Black pepper (as desired)
- Sea salt (as desired)
- Olive oil (2 T)
- Garlic (1 clove chopped)
- Lemon juice (1 lemon)
- Lemon zest (.5 lemons)
- Cumin (.25 tsp.)
- Tahini (.3 c)
- Garbanzo beans (.5 lbs.)
- Garlic powder (.5 tsp.)
- Water (3.5 c)

What to Do
- Add the salt, beans, garlic powder and water to the Instant Pot and mix well. Secure the lid, select high pressure and cook on manual mode for 1 hour.
- Wait for the pressure to decrease naturally before draining the beans while retaining the cooking liquid to use when making the hummus.
- Wait for the beans to cool enough to handle before placing them, .5 c cooking liquid, cumin, salt, olive oil, pepper, lemon zest, lemon juice and tahini in a food processor and process well.
- Check the hummus consistency and add more cooking liquid as needed.

Mashed Squash

Total Prep & Cooking Time: 25 minutes
Yields: 4 Servings

What to Use
- Black pepper (as desired)
- Sea salt (as desired)
- Brown sugar (2 T)
- Coconut oil (2 T)
- Nutmeg (.5 tsp. grated)
- Baking soda (.25 tsp.)
- Kosher salt (1 tsp.)
- Water (.5 c)
- Acorn squash (2 seeded, halved, trimmed)

What to Do
- Add the squash, baking soda and salt to a pressure.
- Add in the pressure cooker cooking rack along with .5 c water along with layers of squash.
- Secure the lid and turn the pressure to high, on a high temperature and allow the squash to cook about 20 minutes. Quick release the pressure and remove the squash from the cooker and place it in a large bowl.
- Scrape the squash flesh into the bowl before adding in the brown sugar, nutmeg and coconut oil.
- Mash the sweet potato using a potato masher. Check the flavor and season as desired prior to serving.

Pesto With Parsley And Cilantro

Total Prep & Cooking Time: 20 minutes
Yields: 4 Servings

What to Use
- Parsley (1 c)
- Lemon juice (.5 lemon)
- Cilantro (1 c packed loosely)
- Almonds (2 T sliced, blanched)
- Extra-virgin olive oil (.25 c)
- Salt (.5 tsp.)

What to Do
- Add half the olive oil, salt, cilantro, parsley, almonds and lemon juice to a blender and pulse to blend.
- Lower the blender speed and add the rest of the olive oil slowly. Blend until the pesto reaches your desired consistency.

Sprout Chips

Total Prep & Cooking Time: 20 minutes
Yields: 2 Servings

What to Use
- Black pepper (as desired)
- Sea salt (as desired)
- Lemon zest (as desired)
- Coconut oil (2 T melted)
- Brussel sprout leaves (2 c)

What to Do
- Ensure your oven is heated to 350 degrees F.
- Coat the leaves using the coconut oil before seasoning as desired and placing them on a baking sheet that has been prepared using parchment paper. Ensure the leaves lay flat in a single layer when you are finished.
- Place the baking sheet in the oven and let the leaves cook about 10 minutes or until the leaves are brown but crispy on the edges.

Cabbage Wedges

Total Prep & Cooking Time: 30 minutes
Yields: 6 Servings

What to Use
- Black pepper (as desired)
- Sea salt (as desired)
- Avocado oil (.5 T)
- Cabbage wedges (1 head of cabbage)
- Lemon wedges (2 lemons)

What to Do
- Ensure your oven is heated to 450 degrees F.
- Place the cabbage on a baking sheet before brushing each wedge with oil to prevent it from burning. Try to keep everything covered evenly for the best result. Leave room between the wedges to ensure they get nice and crispy in the oven.
- Season as desired before placing the baking sheet in the oven for about 15 minutes. Remove the baking sheet, flip the wedges and return the baking sheet to the oven for an additional 10 minutes. You will know they are ready when the edges are crisp but the insides are still tender.
- Garnish with lemon.

Mashed Cauliflower

Total Prep & Cooking Time: 20 minutes
Yields: 4 Servings

What to Use
- Black pepper (as desired)
- Sea salt (as desired)
- Coconut oil (2 T)
- Cauliflower (2 lbs. florets)
- Romano cheese (.5 c)
- Rosemary (2 tsp. dried)
- Chives (to taste)

What to Do
- Add .25 in. water to a frying pan before placing it on the stove over a burner turned to a high heat. Mix in .5 tsp. salt along with the cauliflower florets.
- Cover the pan and allow the cauliflower to steam for about 3 minutes if you like it crisp and 8 minutes if you prefer it soft.
- Drain the cauliflower and add it to a bowl before using a potato masher to mash them along with the coconut oil.
- Add the cheese and any seasonings prior to serving.

Oven Fries

Total Prep & Cooking Time: 40 minutes
Yields: 8 Servings

What to Use
- Black pepper (as desired)
- Sea salt (as desired)
- Coconut oil (3 T)
- Sweet potatoes (2 stripped)
- Garlic powder (2 tsp.)
- Grainy mustard (3 T)
- Purple carrots (halved, quartered)

What to Do
- Pace two baking sheets in the oven and ensure your oven is heated to 450 degrees F.
- Add the sweet potatoes and carrots to a bowl before coating well using the coconut oil and topping with black pepper, salt and garlic. Add the results evenly in single layers to the two baking sheets.
- Bake about 15 minutes before removing the baking sheets from the oven and tossing the fries to ensure they cook evenly. Return the baking sheets to the oven and cook an additional 15 minutes.
- While the fries are cooking add the pepper, sour cream and mustard to a small bowl and mix well.
- Serve fries with a side of dip.

Basil Pesto

Total Prep & Cooking Time: 20 minutes
Yields: 4 Servings

What to Use
- Sea salt (as desired)
- Coconut oil (.5 c)
- Parmesan cheese (.5 c grated)
- Garlic (2 cloves)
- Basil (2 c)

What to Do
- Add all of the ingredients, along with half of the coconut oil to a blender and pulse to blend.
- Lower the speed of the blender and slowly add the remaining oil in and blend until it reaches your desired texture.

Sage Pesto

Total Prep & Cooking Time: 20 minutes
Yields: 4 Servings

What to Use
- Black pepper (as desired)
- Sea salt (as desired)
- Extra-virgin olive oil (.25 c)
- Garlic (1 clove minced)
- Sage leaves (1 c)

What to Do
- Add all of the ingredients, along with half of the coconut oil to a blender and pulse to blend.
- Lower the speed of the blender and slowly add the remaining oil in and blend until it reaches your desired texture.

Braised Carrots With Kale

Total Prep & Cooking Time: 30 minutes
Yields: 2 Servings

What to Use
- Black pepper (as desired)
- Sea salt (as desired)
- Onion (1 sliced thin)
- Chicken bone broth (.5 c)
- Coconut oil (1 T)
- Balsamic vinegar (1 T)
- Garlic (5 cloves chopped, peeled)
- Carrots (3 sliced)
- Kale (10 oz. chopped rough)

What to Do
- Set your Instant Pot to a medium heat and activate the sauté option before adding in your coconut oil. Once it has melted, add in the carrots and onions and let them cook about 5 minutes before adding in the garlic and cooking an additional 30 seconds. Add in the kale, broth and seasonings and mix well.
- Change the Instant Pot setting to manual and set the pot to cook 5 minutes. Secure the lid and allow the pressure to decrease naturally for about 10 minutes before activating the quick release valve.
- Remove the lid from the Instant Pot before adding in the vinegar and mixing well.
- Top with red pepper flakes for a bit of spice.

Beef Bone Broth

Total Prep & Cooking Time: 185 minutes
Yields: 16 Servings

What to Use
- Purified water (4 quarts)
- Apple cider vinegar (2 T)
- Salt (2 tsp.)
- Parsley (2 tsp. dried, crushed)
- Garlic (1 clove crushed)
- Ginger (1 tsp.)
- Lemon rind (2 tsp. ground)
- Yellow onions (2 chopped)
- Carrots (4 chopped)
- Celery (3 stalks chopped)
- Bouquet garni (1 tied with cooking twine)
- Meaty ribs (3 lbs.)
- Bone marrow (2 lbs.)
- Knuckle bones (2 lbs.)

What to Do
- Roast the bones prior to making a stock for the best results.
- Add the knuckle bones, bone marrow, meaty ribs, bouquet garni, celery, carrots, yellow onions, lemon rind, ginger, apple cider vinegar and garlic to a large stockpot.
- Add in the water and let everything sit for 30 minutes to give the apple cider vinegar time to do its thing.
- Add the pot to the stove over a burner turned to a high heat before letting it boil. Reduce the heat and allow the pot to simmer for 180 minutes.
- 10 minutes before the stock has finished cooking, add in the salt as well as the parsley.

- Strain the stock prior to cooling or serving and save the results for another meal. Remember, fattier stocks will need a sturdy wire strainer.

Cajun Greens

Total Prep & Cooking Time: 35 minutes
Yields: 4 Servings

What to Use
- Black pepper (as desired)
- Sea salt (as desired)
- Onion (1 c chopped)
- Turnip (1 c chopped)
- Mustard (1 c chopped)
- Kale (1 c chopped)
- Collard greens (1 c chopped)
- Spinach (1 c chopped)
- Bacon fat (1 T)
- Garlic (2 cloves crushed)
- Ham (1 lb. cooked, chunked,
- Chicken bone broth (.5 c)

What to Do
- Add all of the ingredients to your Instant Pot, secure the lid, set the timer for 20 minutes and select the manual option after choosing high pressure.
- Allow the pressure to release manually for 10 minutes before venting the rest.
- Mix results together for flavor and serve.

Chickpea Trail Mix

Total Prep & Cooking Time: 17 minutes
Yields: 5 Servings

What to Use
- Black pepper (as desired)
- Sea salt (as desired)
- Cajun season (1 T)
- Ginger (1 inch ground)
- Cashews (.5 c)
- Chickpeas (1 c)
- Coconut oil (2 T)
- Raw honey (.5 c)
- Mango (6 oz. dried)
- Water (1 T)
- Almonds (1 c)
- Pecans (1.5 c halved)

What to Do
- Ensure your oven is heated to 375 degrees F.
- Add all of the ingredients save the coconut oil to your Instant Pot and mix well.
- Turn the Instant Pot to sauté and coat everything in the coconut oil and honey. After it has sautéed for a few minutes if it seems to thick or sticky add in the extra 1 T of water.
- Turn the pressure cooker to the manual setting and a high pressure and let it cook for 10 minutes, using the quick release pressure valve at that time.
- Spread the results on a baking sheet lined with parchment paper and place the baking sheet in the oven for 5 minutes, remove the baking sheet, toss the nuts and turn the sheet and return it to the oven for an additional few minutes, taking care not to burn the nuts.

- Remove the baking sheet from the oven and allow it to cool before adding in the mango. Pour the trail mix into an air tight container and shake well to combine.

Steamed Artichokes

Total Prep & Cooking Time: 25 minutes
Yields: 2 Servings

What to Use
- Black pepper (as desired)
- Sea salt (as desired)
- Lemon wedge (1)
- Artichoke (2)
- Water (1 c)

What to Do
- Rinse the artichokes before removing any damaged leaves as well as the stems using a sharp knife. From there, remove roughly the top third of the artichoke and then rub it with a lemon wedge to prevent it from browning in the heat.
- Set the basket in your Instant Pot before adding in your artichoke and the water. Seal the Instant Pot and set it to a high pressure in manual mode. The size of your artichoke will determine the cooking time with small artichokes cooking for 5 minutes, medium artichokes cooking for 10 minutes and large artichokes cooking for 15 minutes.
- All the pressure to release naturally for 10 minutes before using the manual release option.

Pork Stew With Pineapple

Total Prep & Cooking Time: 130 minutes
Yields: 6 Servings

What to Use
- Black pepper (as desired)
- Sea salt (as desired)
- Kumquat jam (2 T)
- Cloves (.5 tsp. ground)
- Bay leaf (1)
- Garlic (2 cloves chopped)
- Pineapple chunks (1 c)
- Turmeric powder (.5 tsp.)
- Cinnamon (1 tsp.)
- Cassava flour (.25 c)
- Ginger powder (.5 tsp.)
- Pork (2 lb. cubed)
- Coconut aminos (1 T)
- Bacon fat (2 T)
- Chard (1 bunch)
- Onion (1 wedged)
- Pork bone broth (1 c)

What to Do
- Turn your Instant Pot to Sauté and allow it to heat fully before adding in the fat and the onions and letting them cook about 5 minutes before adding in the garlic and letting it cook an additional 3 minutes before removing the garlic and onions from the Instant Pot and setting them aside.
- Add in some coconut oil if needed before adding in the porn and letting it brown. Return the garlic and onion to the pot before adding in the kumquat jam, cinnamon and bay leaf.

- Seal the Instant Pot and select the Stew option to set the timer for 35 minutes. When time is up, use the quick release option.
- Remove the lit and adjust the setting to sauté once more before adding in the chard.
- Discard the bay leaf and season as desired prior to serving.

Chicken Bone Broth

Total Prep & Cooking Time: 48 hours
Yields: 8 cups

What to Use
- 3 chicken carcasses
- 1 tablespoon of apple cider vinegar
- 1 bay leaf
- 2 onions
- 1 clove of garlic
- 2 tablespoons of peppercorns
- 3 celery stalks
- 3 carrots
- Parsley
- Thyme

What to Do
- Assemble all of the ingredients and place them in the crockpot (a 6-quart crockpot will hold all of the items plus the 2.5 quarts of water required).
- Set the crockpot on a low setting and cook for 24 to 48 hours.
- If you are interested in straining out the excess fat pour the contents through a wire strainer before cooling and storing.
- Note on storing, if your broth doesn't gel as discussed it is most likely because you added to much water, cut back next time to increase the nutritional value per cup.

Fish Bone Broth

Total Prep & Cooking Time: 24 hours
Yields: 8 cups

What's to Use
- Sea salt (to taste)
- Fish bones (2 lbs.)
- Apple Cider Vinegar (1 T)
- Water (3 quarts)

What to Do
- Place all of the items in a crockpot (6-quart or more)
- Place the crockpot on a low setting for about 24 hours, during this period foam will rise to the top which you want to remove as it contains impurities.
- When finished strain the broth with a wire strainer
- Cool and store

Turkey Bone Broth

Total Prep & Cooking Time: 48 hours
Yields: 8 cups

What to Use
- 1 large turkey carcass
- 1 tbsp. of apple cider vinegar
- 2 tbsps. of black pepper
- 2 leaves of bay
- 2 stalks of celery (2-inch pieces)
- 1 clove of garlic (halved)
- 1 onion (quartered)
- 1 leek (2-inch pieces)
- 2 carrots (2-inch pieces)

What to Do
1. Assemble all of the ingredients and place them in the crockpot (a 6-quart crockpot will hold all of the items plus the 2.5 quarts of water required).
2. Set the crockpot on a low setting and cook for 24 to 48 hours.
3. If you are interested in straining out the excess fat pour the contents through a wire strainer before cooling and storing.

Jicama Fries

Total Prep & Cooking Time: 70 minutes
Yields: 4 Servings

What to Use
- Black pepper (as desired)
- Sea salt (as desired)
- Paprika (1 dash)
- Chili powder (1 tsp.)
- Garlic powder (.5 tsp.)
- Onion powder (.5 tsp.)
- Coconut oil (3 T)
- Jicama (1 lb.)

What to Do
- Ensure your oven is heated to 400 degrees F.
- Peel and slice the jicama so that the end result resembles a bowl of French fries.
- Add the jicama to a pot and fill it with water and a pinch of salt before placing it on the stove over a burner turned to a high heat. Allow the jicama to boil for about 15 minutes before removing from the pot and patting dry.
- Place the jicama on a baking sheet in an even layer and coat with the coconut oil.
- Combine the salt, pepper, onion, garlic and chili powder and mix well before using the results to coat the fries.
- Place the baking sheet in the oven for 20 minutes, remove the baking sheet and flip the fries before returning the baking sheet to the oven for another 20 minutes.
- Let them cool about 5 minutes prior to serving.

Chapter 7: Dessert Recipes

Cassava

Total Prep & Cooking Time: 35 minutes
Yields: 4 Servings

What to Use
- Goat's milk kefir (1.25 c)
- Vanilla extract (.5 tsp.)
- Coconut oil (3 T)
- Cinnamon (1 tsp.)
- Sea salt (.25 tsp.)
- Nutmeg (1 pinch)
- Eggs (2)
- Baking powder (1 T)
- Water (.25 c)
- Monk's fruit sweetener (2 T)
- Cassava flour (1 c)

What to Do
- Place a nonstick griddle on the stove over a burner turned to a low/medium heat.
- In a small bowl, mix together the kefir, water, eggs and vanilla before adding in the coconut oil.
- In a separate bowl, combine the nutmeg, cinnamon, baking powder, sweetener, flour and sea salt and mix well.
- Combine the two bowls and whisk well until the ingredients are thoroughly combined.
- Scoop the batter onto the griddle in .25 c dollops. Cook about 2 minutes per side.

- Top with butter and cinnamon prior to serving.

Balsamic Strawberry Sauce

Total Prep & Cooking Time: 25 minutes
Yields: 2 Servings

What to Use
- Water (.25 c)
- Raw honey (.25 c)
- Frozen strawberries (16 oz.)
- Balsamic vinegar (2 T)

What to Do
- Add the water and strawberries to a saucepan before placing it on the stove over a burner turned to a low heat. Allow it to reduce and melt the strawberries while stirring, until it forms a glaze.
- In the same saucepan add in the honey and balsamic vinegar and cook an additional 15 minutes.
- Add the results to an immersion mixer and mix until smooth.
- Return the mixture to the saucepan and turn the burner to a medium heat to allow the sauce to thicken. Stir regularly until it reaches the desired consistency before pouring it into a mason jar and placing it in the refrigerator to cool.

Cake in a mug

Total Prep & Cooking Time: 3 minutes
Yields: 1 serving

What to Use
- Sea salt (1 pinch)
- Seasonal fruit (1 T)
- Tiger nut flour (1 T)
- Coconut flour (1 T)
- Coconut oil (2 T)
- Egg (1 beaten)
- Baking powder (.5 tsp.)
- Monk fruit sweetener (.5 tsp.)
- Vanilla (.5 tsp.)

What to Do
- In a mug that is microwave safe, combine the vanilla, salt, sweetener, baking powder, tiger nut flour, coconut flour and oil and mix well.
- Add in the egg and use a fork to beat the batter until it is smooth. Scrape down the sides and the bottom to ensure the cake doesn't stick. Finally, fold in the fruit.
- Add the mug to the microwave and let it cook for 90 seconds.
- Allow the cake to cool 60 seconds before removing it from the mug.

Lectin-Free Yogurt

Total Prep & Cooking Time: 25 minutes
Yields: 4 Servings

What to Use
- Coconut milk (27 oz.
- Probiotic capsules (2)
- Vanilla extract (1 tsp.)
- Raw honey (2 T)

What to Do
- Place the coconut milk in the refrigerator overnight to give the milk time to separate from the cream.
- Open the cans and scrape the cream into a bowl before adding in the probiotic capsules after breaking them open. Add in the vanilla and honey and blend thoroughly.
- Divide between an appropriate number of glass jars before placing each jar in your yogurt maker and following the relevant instructions. Allow the finished product to it at least 15 hours. The longer it is allowed to ferment, the sourer the end product will be.

Green Smoothie

Total Prep & Cooking Time: 15 minutes
Yields: 2 Servings

What to Use
- Mint leaves (2 T)
- Ginger root (1 T chopped)
- Banana (1 chopped)
- Avocado (.5)
- Lime juice (1 T)
- Chard (.5 c)
- Spinach (1 c)
- Kale (.5 c)
- Sea salt (1 pinch)
- Ice cubes (4)
- Sparkling water (16 fl. oz.)

What to Do
- Chill the sparkling water
- Add all of the ingredients to a blender and select the puree option before blending for one minute or until smooth. If the results are too thick to drink readily add additional sparkling water to thin as desired.

Chocolate Cherry Cupcakes

Total Prep & Cooking Time: 75 minutes
Yields: 18 Servings

What to Use
- Tart cherry juice (.25 c + .5 T)
- Erythritol (1 c + 1 T)
- Black cherries (1 lb.)
- Sea salt (1 pinch)
- Coconut oil (.25 c)
- Espresso (1 splash)
- Heavy whipping cream (1 c)
- Dark chocolate shavings (.25 c)
- Egg (1)
- Cocoa powder (.3 c)
- Lemon juice (1 T)
- Salt (.5 tsp.)
- Coconut oil (.25 c)
- Baking soda (.75 tsp.)
- Monk fruit sweetener (.5 c)
- Cassava flour (.75 c)
- Vanilla extract (.5 tsp)
- Coconut milk (.75 c)

What to Do
- Separate 20 cherries from the rest and set aside. Add the rest of the cherries to a large bowl before adding in .25 c tart cherry juice and allowing them to soak overnight.
- Ensure your oven is heated to 350 degrees F.
- Grease a large cupcake tin using coconut oil

- In a mixing bowl, combine the vinegar and coconut milk and let it sit for 10 minutes.
- Use a sieve to add the salt, cocoa powder, flour and baking soda together in a separate bowl.
- In a third bowl, combine the sweetener and the cream until blended well before adding in the eggs and combining thoroughly.
- Alternate between adding wet and dry ingredients to the milk and vinegar mixture, taking care to ensure everything is well-mixed.
- Add the resulting batter to the cupcake cups so that they are each about 75 percent full to give them room to expand as they bake.
- Add the cupcake tin to the oven for 20 minutes. You will know the cupcakes are done if you can stick a toothpick into the middle cupcake and pull it out clean.
- To make the filling, beat the butter in a mixing bowl until it is nice and creamy before adding in the salt, espresso and sweetener. Add in the cherry juice 1 T at a time to thin out the mixture as needed.
- Cut each cupcake in half before adding cherry juice and filling to each cupcake, along with one of the reserved cherries. Return the removed cupcake half to make a cupcake sandwich.
- Make the frosting by taking any remaining cherry juice and whipping it with vanilla and crema sweetener in a mixing bowl. Add the results to a pastry bag to decorate the cupcakes.

Instant Pot Applesauce

Total Prep & Cooking Time: 30 minutes
Yields: 4 Servings

What to Use
- Apples (12 cored, diced)
- Apple cider (.5 c)

What to Do
- Place the apples in the Instant Pot before adding in the apple cider which will prevent the apples from getting too dry in the pot which will ultimately make it easier to make them into a sauce.
- Cut holes out of a large piece of parchment paper such that it will fit over the inner rim of the Instant Pot and place it on top of the apples to ensure they retain as much heat as possible.
- Seal the lid on the Instant Pot, set it to manual and set the time to 10 minutes. Allow the pressure to release naturally when the time is up.
- Using an immersion blender, blend the apples until they reach your desired consistency.
- Pour the apple sauce into mason jars and cool prior to serving.

Strawberry Shortcake

Total Prep & Cooking Time: 60 minutes
Yields: 8 Servings

What to Use
- Tiger nut flour (.3 c)
- Baking soda (.75 tsp.)
- Fine sea salt (.5 tsp.)
- Golden monk fruit (.25 c)
- Vanilla extract (.5 tsp.)
- Eggs (3)
- Coconut oil (8 T)
- Coconut cream (.5 c)
- Arrowroot starch (3 T)
- Lemon zest (.5 lemons)
- Coconut flour (.3 c)
- Strawberries (1 qt. sliced, hulled)
- Vanilla extract (.5 tsp.)
- Raw honey (1 T)
- Heavy cream (1 c)

What to Do
- Ensure your oven is heated to 350 degrees F.
- Grease a round cake pan (8 in.) using coconut oil before lining it with parchment paper. Finally, grease it again before coating the grease in a light sprinkling of flour.
- With the help of a stand mixer, combine the coconut oil, coconut cream and sweeteners before adding in the eggs, vanilla extract and lemon zest and blending well to combine thoroughly.
- In a separate bowl, combine the sea salt, tiger nut flour, arrowroot starch, coconut flour and baking soda and mix

well before adding it to the mixer mixture and blending on a low speed until smooth.
- Add the batter to the baking pan, ensuring the top is smooth and bubble free. Tapping the pan on the counter will help to release trapped air bubbles and settle the batter.
- Place the pan in the oven for about 25 minutes or until you can stick a knife into the center of the cake and pull it out clean.
- Remove the cake from the oven and allow it to cool for 30 minutes before removing it from the pan and placing it on a rack where you are to allow it to continue to cool until it reaches room temperature.
- With the help of the stand mixer, combine the cream, honey and vanilla extract at high speed until peaks begin to form.
- Frost the cake prior to serving.

Blueberry Dessert

Total Prep & Cooking Time: 60 minutes
Yields: 4 Servings

What to Use
- Whipping cream (8 oz.)
- Xylitol (3 T divided)
- Salt (1 pinch)
- Vanilla extract (.5 tsp.)
- Blueberries (2 c)
- Lemon (.5 zested, juiced)
- Heavy cream (1.3 c)

What to Do
- Add the salt, 1.5 c blueberries and 2 T xylitol into a boiler set to a medium heat and let everything heat until it begins to bubble. Reduce the temperature to low and stir constantly for 5 minutes.
- Remove the boiler from heat before adding in the rest of the blueberries, lemon zest and lemon juice and mix well before allowing the mixture to reach room temperature.
- While waiting for this to occur, combine the xylitol, vanilla and heavy whipping cream in a small bowl and whisk well to combine thoroughly. Continue whisking until it begins to form peaks before folding in the blueberry sauce gently.
- Divide into serving dishing and top with blueberries and chocolate shavings.

Mug Gingerbread

Total Prep & Cooking Time: 15 minutes
Yields: 4 Servings

What to Use
- Cinnamon (.25 tsp.)
- Water (.5 T)
- Raw honey (2 tsp.)
- Tiger nut (1 T)
- Baking powder (.5 tsp.)
- Coconut flour (1 T)
- Coconut oil (1 T)
- Ground ginger (.5 tsp.)
- Apple cider vinegar (.5 tsp.)
- Cloves (1 pinch)
- Nutmeg (1 pinch)
- Allspice (1 pinch)
- Egg (1 beaten)

What to Do
- In a mug that is microwave safe, combine all the ingredients save the egg and mix well.
- Add in the egg and use a fork to beat the batter until it is smooth. Scrape down the sides and the bottom to ensure the cake doesn't stick. Finally, fold in the fruit.
- Add the mug to the microwave and let it cook for 90 seconds.
- Allow the cake to cool 60 seconds before removing it from the mug.

Ginger Cake

Total Prep & Cooking Time: 60 minutes
Yields: 12 Servings

What to Use
- Sea salt (.25 tsp.)
- Coconut oil (.25 c softened)
- Pumpkin pie spice (2 tsp.)
- Ginger (.5 tsp. ground)
- Vanilla extract (2 tsp. divided)
- Baking soda (.75 tsp.)
- Almond flour (.3 c)
- Erythritol (.5 c)
- Cassava flour (.75 c)
- Eggs (2)
- Baking powder (.5 tsp.)
- Cream cheese (4 oz. softened)
- Confectioners erythritol (.75 c)

What to Do
- Ensure your oven is heated to 300 degrees F and your oven rack is set to the center of your oven.
- Grease a glass pan (9 x 13) with coconut oil.
- Combine the coconut milk and apple cider vinegar in a measuring cup and mix well before setting aside.
- In a mixing bowl, combine the salt, baking soda, ginger, flour and pumpkin pie spice and whisk well.
- In a separate bowl, beat the eggs with the coconut oil and sugar before adding in the vanilla and coconut milk and mixing well.
- Combine the two bowls and use a spatula to stir. The batter should be very thick.

- Add the cake batter to a greased pan and use a spatula to ensure it spreads easily. Tap the pan to remove any air bubbles.
- Place the pan in the oven for about 40 minutes. You will know its ready when you can stick a knife in the center and pull it out clean.
- For the icing, start by beating together the cream cheese and erythritol at a slow speed before adding in the vanilla extract and blending well. You will want the end result to be thin enough to spread with a knife but no so thin that it drips off the knife. If it is too thick to start you can thin it out by adding 1 T of water at a time until it reaches your desired thickness.
- Frost the cake and top with cinnamon.

Mint Pesto

Total Prep & Cooking Time: 20 minutes
Yields: 4 Servings

What to Use
- Sliced almonds (.25 c blanced0
- Coconut oil (3 T divided)
- Mint leaves (1 c packed loose)
- Raw honey (.25 c)

What to Do
- Add all of the ingredients save 2 T coconut oil to a blender and pulse well until thoroughly combined.
- Slowly add in the remaining coconut oil while blending at a slow speed. Continue blending until your desired texture is reached.

Peach Cobbler

Total Prep & Cooking Time: 40 minutes
Yields: 4 Servings

What to Use
- Peaches (2 sliced thin)
- Baking soda (.25 tsp.)
- Baking powder (.25 tsp.)
- Fine sea salt (.25 tsp.)
- Cassava flour (.25 c)
- Goat's milk kefir (5 oz.)
- Liquid stevia (5 drops)
- Coconut flour (.25 c)
- Coconut oil (1 T)
- Vanilla extract (1 tsp.)
- Tapioca flour (.25 c)
- Egg (2)

What to Do
- Ensure your oven is heated to 350 degrees F.
- In a mixing bowl, beat the eggs, kefir, stevia and vanilla together and mix well before adding in the coconut oil and whisking steadily to prevent it from solidifying.

- Mix in the baking soda, baking powder, sea salt, cassava flour, tapioca flour and coconut flour and mix well. Whisk steadily until the batter is fully smooth.
- Add the results to a pie pan before placing half of the peaches into a single layer on top before seasoning with cinnamon.
- Place the pie tin in the oven for 30 minutes, you will know it is ready when you can stick a toothpick into the center of the pie and pull it out clean.
- Top with remaining peach slices prior to serving.

Conclusion

When you are first making the transition to the lectin-free diet, it is important to always keep in mind that it isn't all or nothing. That is to say, just because you may find yourself in a situation where you aren't able to make a lectin-free choice, doesn't mean that you are somehow failing at the lectin-free diet. On the contrary, every single meal where you actively decrease the amount of lectin in your diet is a win and every meal where this doesn't happen is simply a chance to do better next time. As long as you don't let a single mistake turn into a prolonged binge of unhealthy foods full of lectin then there is nothing to hang your head about when you step out of line. Just remember, following the lectin-free diet is a marathon, not a sprint which means slow and steady will always win the race.

Part 2

Introduction

What Is Plant Paradox And Is It Healthy?

As more people are becoming diet conscious, thus more research is being conducted in order to come up with foods that offer the best of both worlds. These researches aid people to avoid foods that might seem tempting now, but have negative effects in the end.

Many of us are familiar with a protein, gluten, present in wheat. Gluten tends to cause inflammation in the human body. However, according to Dr. Steve Gundry's discovery, gluten is one variety of a highly toxic protein found in plants. This common plant-based protein is called Lectin. You can find lectin in almost 30 percent of the food that you eat. Lectin is a carbohydrate-binding protein, thus when it binds to different carbohydrates in different foods it tends to have a different impact.

Where To Find Lectin

Lectin is readily available, in plants, it is mostly present in seed coats or first leave of a sprouting plant also known as cotyledon. In lame man terms, we can say that lectin is the defense mechanism that plants tend to use against predators. Lectin keeps the insects at bay, thus allowing the plant to flourish. Besides plant, the lectin is also available in animals.

Disadvantages Of Lectin

Although for decades scientist has been using lectin to help molecules and cells stick together. However, consuming excessive of anything is bad. According to the latest research, consuming a large amount of lectin will have an adverse effect on your health. Lectin passes through the stomach unaltered. Once it reaches the intestine, it has the ability to attach itself to the gut lining leading to digestive problems. In addition, frequently eating lectin can also result in chronic illness.

Lectins are anti-nutrients it means that in taking a good amount of it can affect your body's ability to absorb nutrients. If you eat plants that contain lectin without cooking, it can lead to an upset stomach. For instance, red beans are rich with lectin and when you eat them without cooking there is a high possibility that you suffer from food poisoning. Lectin hinders your efforts to lose weight. Lectin sugar binding and is present in almost every plant and some animals. When you consume plants and animals rich with lectin, you are unable to lose weight.

According to a study published in the British Journal of nutrition by Colorado State University's Health and Exercise Science, lectins play a role in autoimmune conditions including rheumatoid arthritis. When the immune system of the body starts to attack the healthy cells, it is called autoimmune condition. This results in chronic pain, fatigue and inflammation.

These are some issues associated with a diet high in lectin. There are numerous other disadvantages including severe abdominal pain, diarrhea, vomiting and much more.

The only way to avoid all these issues is to change your diet to a lectin free-diet. However, the important question here is, when almost 30 percent of the foods both animals and plants have lectin, how can you avoid it. It is here where we come in handy. In the course of this book, we will be telling you about how to rid your diet of lectin. We will shed light on different lectin free-cooking recipes, shopping list and many more.

Plant Paradox Kitchen: Foods Allowed in Lectin-free Diet

To maintain a healthy lifestyle, it is important that you watch your diet. A lectin-free diet is an elimination diet. It focuses on foods that have a small amount of lectin in them. Mostly, you will cruciferous vegetables, fish; pasture-raised meats are low on lectin. Consuming them in your diet is the best way to lead a healthy life.

Below we have come up with a list of foods that you can eat in a lectin-free diet.

Vegetables

A good lectin-free diet mainly compromises of leafy vegetables. Some common vegetables that you can add to your diet include fennel, parsley, Kohlrabi, lettuce, spinach, romaine, and endive. Also, there are certain vegetables that you can eat after steaming or bowling such as Brussels sprouts, kale, and broccoli. Other options include asparagus, cucumber, celery, onions, and garlic.

Protein

It is imperative to take around 30 grams of protein in the morning. In case you are suffering from any sort of chronic inflammatory disease or any other autoimmune disease, make sure that your diet incorporates around 20 to 30 percent of protein.

- Fish: It is low on lectin, but high on protein. There are different low-toxicity kinds of seafood, but we believe anchovies, oysters, roe, fresh wild sardines, and wild-caught salmon to be the best.
- Meat: In terms of meat, you need to choose wisely. It is preferable for you to eat grass-fed beef. You can eat chicken, however, avoid the sharp bone fragments.
- Pork
- Cooked Tempeh
- Glycine
- Nutritional yeast
- Brewer's yeast
- Bone Broth
- Liver
- Hemp Protein
- Cricket Flour

Fats

For the oils, we suggest that you use black cumin seed oil, caprylic acid, extra virgin olive oil, and also ghee. It is important that you cut out omega-6 oils.

In order to avoid any gastrointestinal effects, you should try to have a couple of tablespoons of caprylic oil. It is important that you space them right. In addition, take about one tablespoon of extra virgin olive oil as well as black cumin seed oil daily. Other fats that you can eat include Avocados, Avocados oil, Hemp seeds. Keep in mind that not everyone can tolerate hemp seeds, so if they cause trouble to you, stop eating them.

Carbs

- If you are looking for something sweet, we believe raw honey is the best carb that you can take. Other carbs include starch. You can find starch in sweet potatoes and Japanese sweet potatoes. You need to make sure that they are well cooked.
- In terms of fruit, you can have mango, mulberries, papaya, golden berries, citrus, pineapple, and blueberries.
- Fiber is another important thing. You can use resistant starch.
- Carob and Trehalose are also good forms of fibers.

Condiments And Others

You can add general spices as they are not going to cause much trouble. Below are some important condiments that you can include in your lectin-free diet.

- Nutritional yeast
- Xylitol
- Stevia
- Italian seasoning
- Mustard
- Sunflower lectin
- Dulse Powder
- Nori for iodine

We did come up with a comprehensive list of all the foods that you can have when on a lectin-free diet.

Plant Protein Food: Grain-free Tempeh, Veggie burger, Hemp tofu, Hilary's root, and Quorn

Sweetness: Xylitol, Luo Han Guo, Erythritol, Monk Fruit, Inulin, Yacon, and Stevia

Fruits: All Berries and Avocado

Grass-fed Meat: Prosciutto, Pork, Beef, Lamb, Venison boar, Elk, Bison, and Wild game

Poultry
Chicken, Dove Grouse, goose, egg, Duck, Quail, Ostrich, and Turkey

Starches
It is important that you limit your intake of starches

- Millet sorghum
- Tiger nuts
- Mango
- Taro roots
- Celery root Persimmon
- Glucomannan
- Yucca
- Rutabaga
- Parsnips
- Yams or Sweet Potatoes
- Green Papaya
- Baobab Fruit
- Cassava
- Green plantains
- Green Bananas
- Coconut flour Bagels
- Paleo Coconut Flakes cereal
- Seven brand tortillas
- Coconut Flour bread

Fish

- Canned tuna
- Anchovies
- Sardines
- Calamari
- Mussels
- Oysters
- Scallops
- Crab
- Lobster
- Alaskan Salmon
- Shrimp
- Alaskan halibut
- Hawaiian fish
- Whitefish
- Freshwater bass
- Wild caught fish

Diary

- Organic sour cream
- Buffalo mozzarella
- Organic heavy cream
- Organic cream cheese
- High-fat French/Italian/Switzerland cheese
- Coconut yogurt
- Sheep and Goad Kefir
- Sheep cheese
- Goat Brie
- Goat cheese
- Grass-fed butter
- Goat butter

- Ghee
- Sparingly cheese
- Sparingly Yogurt
- Casein A2 Milk
- Leafy Greens
- Sea vegetables
- Mushrooms
- Seaweed
- Dandelion greens
- Algae
- Perilla
- Mint
- Mizuna
- Parsley
- Purslane
- Basil
- Mustard greens
- Fennel
- Escarole
- Butter lettuce
- Endive
- Spinach
- Kohlrabi
- Mesclun
- Romaine
- Red and green leaf lettuce

Noodles

- Kanten Pasta
- Miracle Rice
- Shirataki Noodles
- Miracle Noodles

- Cappello's Fettuccine
- Pasta Slim

Nuts

- Psyllium
- Dark Chocolate
- Hemp Protein Powder
- Brazil nuts
- Hemp seeds
- Sesame seeds
- Chestnuts
- Flaxseeds
- Pistachios
- Coconut cream hazelnuts
- Coconut
- Walnuts
- Pecans
- Macadamia

Flours

- Tiger nut flour
- Arrowroot
- Grape seed flour
- Green banana flour
- Sweet potato flour
- Cassava flour
- Sesame flour
- Chestnut flour
- Hazelnut flour
- Coconut flour

- Almond flour

Oils

- Sesame oil
- Flavored cod liver oil
- Red palm oil
- Rice bran oil
- Perilla oil
- Walnut oil
- Avocado oil
- Macadamia oil
- MCT oil
- Coconut oil
- Algae oil
- Olive oil

Others

- 1 glass wine in a day
- 1-ounce spirits in a day
- All herbs except chili pepper flakes
- Dairy-free ice cream
- Sugar-free vinegar

To ensure that your diet is low on lectin, below are some foods that you need to avoid. We will also give your comprehensive list of all the foods that you need to avoid.

Red Kidney Beans

Red Kidney beans are high in plant-based protein and fiber, but at the same time, they are also most lectin-rich food out there. A food that is this high in lectin can cause some real damage especially when you eat them raw. Eating even a couple of uncooked red kidney beans can lead to serious stomach issues.

Corn

In order to avoid overly processed grains, one turns toward corn. The food is a healthy source of carbohydrates, but it is also rich with lectin. This means that consuming corn on a regular basis can do more harm than being healthy. So, if you plan to go on a lectin-free diet. It is best that you avoid corn.

Soybeans

Despite offering many advantages, Soybeans are not the best choice for a healthy lectin free diet. We agree that soybeans are rich with protein for plant food. They are also high in nutrients including thiamine and phosphorus, yet they are unhealthy, as they are one of the higher-lectin foods.

If you really want to add soybeans to our diet, it imperative that you pay special attention to the way they are prepared. According to a study, if you fermentation of soybeans can lead to the reduction of lectin content up to 95 percent. However, it is better to eliminate soybeans all together for an effective lectin-free diet.

Wheat

Since wheat is rich in gluten, many people already tend to avoid it. They also avoid the highly processed nature of the wheat such as bread and pasta. Even if you are gluten intolerant, having wheat can lead to problems, as it is high in lectin. Several people have reported that once they leave what they feel light.

Casein A1 Milk

Milk is an imperative part of a healthy diet. We will never tell you to let go of something as important as milk. However, use Casein A2 milk instead of Casein A1. Most on the shelf dairy products contain Casein A1 and that is high in lectin. Sheep milk, goat milk, and cheese made from these milk contain Casein A2, thus they are low on lectin.

Fruits: Out Of Season

Although most fruits a high in lectin, but out of season fruits have a higher level of lectin in comparison with in-season fruits. It is important that you limit your intake of out of season fruits. The best option is that you take only the in-season fruit.

Potatoes

Potatoes are popular because they are their starch carbohydrates. While many people love them, these potatoes are rich in lectin as well. The lectin present in potatoes are also heat-resistant, thus you will have to avoid them all together in order to go lectin-free. According to studies, cooking a potato did not eradicate even forty to fifty percent of lectin.

Peanuts

The name can be deceiving, peanuts are not nuts on the contrary they are legumes. This fact is not very popular among the general audience. Since they are legumes, thus they are high in lectin content. The bad news is that you can't reduce the level of lectin in peanuts as you can't cook them. According to different studies, peanuts are highly rich in lectin. This means which you consume a good number of peanuts you are also in taking lectin. So, it is better than you have walnuts or cashews instead of peanuts.

Squash

Squash seeds and skin are very high in lectins. In case you want to incorporate squash in your diet, it is important that you remove the skin and avoid the seeds. Squash are important, as they are a healthy source of nutrient-rich carbohydrates.

Tomatoes

Tomatoes offer many health benefits. The fruit is rich in lycopene content. The bad news is that it is also high in lectin. However, we did not yet find an authentic study claiming the lectin present in tomatoes passes through the gut into the bloodstream. Yet, it is better to be safe than sorry.

Comprehensive List of Foods to Avoid in Lectin-free Diet

Fruits

- All fruits expect in-season fruit.
- Ripe Bananas
- Goji Berries

Pseudograins, Grasses And Sprouted Grains

- Wheatgrass
- Barely grass
- Spelt
- Corn syrup
- Orn product
- Cornstarch,
- Popcorn
- Corn
- Kasha
- Barley
- Buckwheat

- Brown rice
- Bulgur
- White rice
- Quinoa
- Rye
- Oats
- Wheat Einkorn
- Wheat Kamut
- Whole grains
- Nuts and Seeds
- Cashews
- Peanuts
- Sunflower
- Chia
- Pumpkin
- Soy-fed

Pork

- Lamb
- Beef
- Seafood
- Fish

Oils

- Hydrogenated vegetable oil
- Canola oil
- Sunflower oil
- Cottonseed oil
- Safflower oil
- Peanut oil

- Grapeseed oil
- Corn oil
- Soy oil

Milk Products

- Casein protein powders
- American cheese
- Kefir
- Cottage cheese
- Ricotta
- Greek yogurt
- Frozen yogurts
- Casein a-1 Yogurt

Vegetables

- Textured vegetable
- All sprouts and beans
- Soy protein
- Edamame
- Soy
- Green beans
- Chickpeas
- Legumes
- Peas
- Melons
- Pumpkins
- Squashes
- Chili peppers
- Cucumbers (except peeled and deseeded)
- Bell pepper (except peeled and deseeded)

- Zucchini
- Tomatoes (except peeled and deseeded)

Starchy Foods

- Diet Drinks
- Maltodextrin
- Sweet n Low
- Sunett SweetOne or NutraSweet
- Cereal
- Agave
- Sugar
- Cookies
- Crackers
- Flours from grains and pseudo
- Pastry
- Bread
- Tortillas
- Milk potatoes chips
- Potatoes
- Pasta
- Rice

Ingredients Substitute

- Use Ketchup BBQ Sauce instead of Barbecue Sauce
- Use Duke's Mayonnaise instead of regular mayonnaise
- Use unsweetened almond coconut milk or unsweetened almond milk instead of milk
- Use arrowroot powder instead of cornstarch
- Use Stevia instead of sugar
- Use coconut aminos instead of soy sauce

- Use almond flour instead of wheat flour

How to Reduce Lectin in high-Lectin foods

The good news is that you can still enjoy foods that have lectin in them. You just need to know the right way to cook them. Researchers have shown that cooking, soaking, fermentation, and sprouting reduces lectin level in foods. However, if you want to go completely on a lectin-free diet, then these tips are not effective at all.

It is safe to have certain beans, as they are low in lectin. Moderate lectin varieties include Pinto III cultivars, great northern beans, lupin seeds, broad beans, cowpeas, and rice beans. The lowest and the safest beans include lentils, raw green beans, and Polish pea.

Prep And Cooking Guidance

Remember never eat raw beans as it can lead to some serious problems. To make beans safe to eat follow the steps below.

Soak beans in water containing baking soda for about 12 hours before cooking. We recommend that you change the water every couple of hours.

Rinse The Beans And Discard Soaking Water.

You need to cook the beans on high heat for 15 minutes. Remembering cooking beans on low heat can increase the toxicity level. Do not use dry beans flour, as the microwave cannot effectively reduce the lentic level. It is always best that you use a pressure cooker for the beans.

Potato Optimization For Health Benefits

The lectins present in tomatoes are more resistant to heat in comparison with the ones present in beans. Cooking potatoes will reduce only 40-50 percent, but you can increase the nutritional value by chilling the potatoes after cooking them. Researchers have shown that when you cook and freeze the potatoes it leads to increased digestive resistant starch. Thus, increasing the health benefits of the potato.

Safe Lectins

When it comes to planting foods, lectin including onions, mushrooms, celery, garlic, and asparagus is a safe option for eating a lectin-free diet. Remember, these foods will contain lectin, but cooking them properly will decrease its level.

Peeling Of Fruits And Vegetables

Removing the seeds and skin of fruits and vegetables decreases the amount of lectin drastically. For instance, if you are on a lectin-restrict diet you can eat almonds after removing their skin.

Sprouting

The lectin content in things decreases by sprouting. However, you need to be careful as there are certain foods that result in higher level of lectin after sprouting. One such example is alfalfa.

Use Pressure Cooker

A pressure cooker is an effective way to reduce plant lectin. According to studies, beans cooked in pressure cooker have 59% less lectin in comparison with the ones that you boil regularly.

Fermenting

Besides reducing the lectin level, fermenting often helps is getting rid of the harmful lectin. You should use only soy fermented products. In the case of bread, the best option is sourdough. In addition, fermenting all vegetables will increase their nutritional value.

Recipes

Morning Meals

Cinnamon Pancakes- Lectin-Free

Serving: 2
Cook Time: 15 minutes
Preparation time: 20 minutes

Ingredients

- Water ¼ cup
- Eggs 2 big
- Melted butter 3 tbsps
- Almond yogurt room temperature ¼ cup
- Vanilla extract ½ tsp
- Sea salt ¼ Tsp
- Nutmeg 1/8 Tsp
- Baking powder 1 tbsp
- Cinnamon 1 Tsp
- Cassava flour 1 cup
- Monk's fruit sweetener 2 tbsps

Preparation

1. Take a nonstick griddle and heat it t med-low.
2. Take a big bowl then add yogurt, vanilla, eggs, and water. Whisk everything until it is fully combined.
3. Take ¼ of batter and scoop onto the hot griddle.
4. Tips: Don't overload, make 1-3 pancake per time

5. Wait till the bottoms of the pancake are golden. This usually takes around 2 minutes.
6. Use a spatula and flip pancakes. Cook for a minute more.
7. Repeat the process for the leftover batter.
8. Serve them hot, sprinkle with butter and cinnamon.

Mexican Black Bean Taco Cups

Cook Time: 45 Minutes
Serving: 12 cups

Ingredients

- Warm water ¼ cup
- Room temperature coconut milk (unsweetened) ½ cup
- Salted palm shortening butter (Melted) ¼ cup
- Olive oil
- Cassava flour 1 cup
- Spicy Black Beans
- Garlic powder ¼ Tsp
- Canned black beans with their liquid
- Dried oregano ½ Tsp
- Paprika ½ Tsp
- Coriander 1 Tsp
- Aminos Coconut 1 Tsp
- Avocado oil 1 Tbsp
- Chili powder 2 Tsp
- Ground cumin 1 Tsp
- Medium onion finely chopped ½

Accompany by

- goat cheddar (grated)
- guacamole
- lettuce (shredded)
- full-fat sour cream

Preparation

1. Heat your oven to 425F

2. Evenly cover 12-cup muffin with grease
3. Take a big bowl, add cassava flour then add some water along with butter and coconut milk. Mix the ingredients well.
4. Divide the mixture into 12 balls 1 oz. each.
5. Roll the balls between two parchment paper pieces.
6. Remove the parchment paper. Once you are done removing, then cover the muffin cup inside the rolled dough.
7. Put the muffin cups in preheated oven. You will have to bake it for almost twenty minutes. Make sure that they are golden brown.
8. Leave the taco cups and wait until they cool down.
9. Take a skillet and add 1 tbsp avocado oil over med-high heat.
10. Now add onions in the skillet and cook until soft. This usually takes about two minutes.
11. After 2 minutes add coconut aminos along with all the spices and cook for another 1 minute.
12. You take the entire mixture and put it in a pressure cooker.
13. Take black beans along with the liquid into the cooker and add sea salt along with lack pepper.
14. Now cook on high pressure for 5 minutes and then release it naturally.
15. Lastly, you need to do the presentation. Take lettuce and place it on top of every cup. Make sure that the layer is thin.
16. Take the beans and top it on the taco cups.
17. Finally, top the cup with hot sauce, guacamole, goat cheddar, and sour cream.

Chocolate Fudge Tarts- Lectin Free

Serves: 3 tarts, 4 inches each
Cook time: 0 minutes
Preparation time: 10 minutes

Ingredients

- Coconut oil 1 tbsp
- Himalayan pink salt 1 pinch
- Walnuts 1 cup
- Pitted Medjool dates 1 cup
- Filling
- Himalayan pink salt 1 pinch
- Date nectar ½ cup
- Raw cacao powder ¼ cup
- Almond butter ½ cup
- Coconut oil ½ cup

Preparation

1. Take a food processor and add every crust ingredient in it.
2. Process crust mixture till you get a wet consistency.
3. Take 3, 4 inches tart molds and evenly split the crust mixture between them.
4. Make sure that there are no spaces underneath.
5. Take a big bowl and add the filling ingredients to it. Whisk until everything is smooth and creamy.
6. Now split filling mixture over crusts.
7. Put the tart molds in the refrigerator until firm. This will take about 1-2 hours.
8. To retain the form of the crust, leave them in the refrigerator until you want to serve them.

Yummy Gingerbread Mug

Serving: 1 person
Cook Time: 1 minute
Preparation Time: 5 minutes

Ingredients

- Large egg 1
- Lime juice ½ tsp
- Water ½ tbsp.
- Nutmeg 1 pinch
- Maple flavored, erythritol syrup 2 tsp
- Allspice 1 pinch
- Cloves 1 pinch
- Ground ginger ½ tsp
- Cinnamon ¼ tsp
- Cassava flour 1 tbsp
- Baking powder ½ tsp
- Softened butter 1 tbsp
- Coconut flour 1 tbsp

Preparation

1. Take an oven-secure mug and put butter, coconut flour, cassava flour, baking powder, ginger, cinnamon, spices, and butter. Beat all the ingredients together.
2. Now add erythritol syrup, lime juice, water, and egg into the mixture and then beat it. You need to beat it until it forms a smooth consistency.
3. Now place mug in the microwave for 1 minute and 30 seconds.
4. Now scrape the mug edges in order to remove gingerbread.
5. Flip and slice the gingerbread into two.
6. Top the sliced bread with butter and cinnamon.

Vanilla Mug Cake- Lectin-Free

Cook time: 1 minute
Preparation Time: 2 Minutes

Ingredients

- Season fruit 1 tbsp
- Sea salt 1 pinch
- Pastured big egg 1 beaten
- Baking powder ½ tsp
- Vanilla ½ tsp
- Tigernut flour 1 tbsp
- Granulated fruit sweetener 2 tsp
- Olive oil 2 tbsps
- Coconut flour 1 tbsp

Method

1. Take an oven secure mug, add olive oil, coconut flour, tiger nut flout, sweetener, baking powder, vanilla, and salt. Combine everything properly.
2. Now take the egg along with the flour and mix it well. You need to beat it until it is smooth.
3. In the scrape mug, fold the seasonal fruit and then heat it for 1 minute and 30 seconds.
4. Leave the mug for 1 minute to cool it.
5. To remove the cake scrape the mug edges and flip it onto the plate.
6. If you prefer, top it with seasonal fruit.

Lime Mousse Tarts

Serves: 4 Person
Cook Time: 0 Times
Preparation Time: 10 minutes

Mousse Ingredients

- Non-GMO xylitol 2 tbsps
- Can coconut milk 1 (13.5oz)
- Squeezed lime juice 2 tbsps

Crust

- Himalayan pink salt 1 pinch
- Coconut oil ½ tbsp.
- Vanilla bean powder 1/8 tsp
- Cup raw pecans ½ cup
- Pitted Medjool dates 2

Preparation

1. Take a food processor and add everything ingredient in it. Blend it until there is a crumbly consistency.
2. Take small silicone muffin cups and add the crust mixture in them. Make sure that the mixture is pressed firmly.
3. Put the muffin cups on a baking sheet and freeze it.
4. Remove the hard coconut fat from the coconut milk that you refrigerated. Leave the water alone.
5. Take a mixer and add hard coconut fat, lime juice and xylitol in it.
6. Mix them well. It is important that you have a fluffy mousse-like consistency, therefore, keep the speed high.
7. Full the mousse filling into the tart crusts.

Snacks And Appetizers

Bagel Thins

Serves: As many people as you like
Cooking time: 10 minutes
Preparation time: 10 minutes

Ingredients

- Grain-free Bagels
- Olive Oil as per required

Preparation

1. We are going to tell you about the different dressing of this amazing and quick to make a snack.
2. Take a grain-free bagel. It is preferable if the bagel is at least a day old.
3. Slice the bagel into thin round pieces. It is better to make slice one bagel into the half.
4. Brush olive oil on it.
5. Bake it for 10 minutes at 325 degrees.
6. For the top layer, you have a variety of dressing.

Prosciutto Manchego
Take a baked bagel slice, apply olive on evenly on it. Then you top it with shredded manchego cheese and prosciutto di Parma.

Garlic Parmesan
Evenly spread butter on it and then top it with crumbled goat cheese. To add more taste put thinly sliced basil leaves.

Cinnamon Sugar

Apply butter evenly and then sprinkle granular and cinnamon sweetener.

Variety Of Dips

You can truly enjoy a lectin free snack if you have the perfect dip with it. Below we have come up with some of the most amazing lectin-free dips.

Lectin Free-Party Hummus

Ingredients

- Frozen cauliflower rice 1 bag
- Juice of 1 lemon
- Cumin 1tsp
- Tahini 2 tbsps
- Garlic clove 1

Preparation

1. Take a food processor and add all the ingredients in it.
2. Process until a thick consistency is formed. If the need arises, you can add water as well.
3.

Vegetarian Low Lectin Hummus

Ingredients

- Canned black beans 1 (15 ounces)
- Cumin 1 tsp
- Juice of 1 lemon
- Tahini 1 tbsps
- Garlic Glove 1

Preparation

1. Cook the canned beans in a pressure cooker and then drain the water.
2. Take a food processor and all the above ingredients in it. Process the ingredients until you get a think consistency. If the need arises, you can add little amount of water as well.

Party Pesto-3

Ingredients

- Grated pecorino romano ¼ cup
- Olive oil ¼ cup
- Fresh basil leaves the ½ cup
- Chopped artichoke hearts ½ cup
- Goat or sheep milk ricotta ½ cup

Preparation

Take a food processor and all the above ingredients in it. Process the ingredients until you get a think consistency. You can serve it with sweet potato chips or celery sticks.

Garlic Salted Rainbow Oven Fries

Serves: 1-2 person
Cooking Time: 20 minutes
Preparation Time: 15-20 Minutes

Ingredients

- Quartered, halved and peeled purple carrots 4
- Peeled yucca roots cut in ¼ inch thick strips 2 medium
- Peeled Sweet potatoes and cut into 1/4 inch thick strips 2 medium
- Extra virgin olive oil 2 tbsps
- Granulated garlic 2 tsp
- Sea salt 2 tsp
- Black pepper as per taste
- Full fat sour cream ¾ cup
- Grainy mustard 3 tbsps

Preparation

1. Start with placing two baking sheets on the bottom and top third of the over. After that, you need to preheat it to 450 degrees F.
2. Take a bag and toss all the ingredients in it. Shake it well to mix everything.
3. Take the sweet potatoes, yucca, and carrots out of the bag and place them between the preheated baking sheets. Sprinkle the spices left in the bag on them as well.
4. You have to bake them for 20 minutes; however, it is important that you toss the fries halfway through.

Dijon Salmon Cake

Serves: 4
Cooking Time: 30 minutes
Preparation Time: 30 minutes

Ingredients

- Dijon mustard 1 tbsp
- Roughly chopped scallions 2
- Skinned Alaskan sock-eye Salmon (Pound Wild) 1
- Black pepper as per taste
- Sea salt as per taste
- Torn fresh mint ¼ cup
- Kalamata olives ½ cup
- Organic vegetable broth 2 cup
- Millet 1 cup
- Olive Oil

Preparation

1. Take a medium saucepan and add broth along with the millet in it. Keep the heat medium-high and boil the mixture. Once it reaches a boiling point, you need to turn the heat to low and simmer. Cover it for 20 minutes.
2. Fold in the ½ teaspoon of salt, pepper, 1 tablespoon of olive oil, mint, and olives.
3. Place Salmon on a paper towel and squeeze out the excess water.
4. Take a food processor and add ¼-teaspoon pepper, ½-teaspoon salt, scallions, and salmon. Blend everything in the food processor until they are finely chopped.
5. Take a big bowl and add salmon long with a ½ cup of cooked Dijon mustard and millet. You should make eight patties.

6. Now take a nonstick skillet and heat it over medium heat. Add 1 tablespoon of oil in it as well. Cook the patties for about 2 minutes per side. Wait until they turn opaque. You can now serve it warm along with the remaining millet or you can put it in the fridge up to three days.

Swiss Chard Fritters

Serves: 4
Cooking time: 30 Minutes
Preparation Time: 30 minutes

Ingredients

- Organic sour cream
- Extra-virgin olive oil 4 tbsps
- Cassava flour ½ cup
- Crumbled goat cheese 2 ounces
- Black pepper as per need
- Sea salt as per need
- Ground cumin ½ tsp
- Chopped garlic cloves 3
- Torn stemmed Swiss Chard 1 bunch

Preparation

1. Take a food processor and add ¼ teaspoon of pepper, ½ teaspoon of salt, cumin, garlic, and swiss chard. Blend all these until you get a finely chopped mixture. If the need arises, you should scrape down the sides of the bowl.
2. Take a large bowl and mix flour, goat cheese and Swiss chard mixture in it.
3. Scoop out the mixture by using a small one-inch ice cream scoop.
4. Flatten the scooped out mixture with hands-on patties. Make sure that these patties are not thicker than ¼ inches.
5. Take a non-stick skillet, add oil to it and heat it over med-high.
6. Now cook patties 3-4 minutes each side. Make sure that the patties sides turn brown before you change it. If you are cooking more than one batch then add two tablespoons of

olive oil for every new batch. You can save the snacks in the fridge for about 5 days.

Soups And Stews

Miso Ramen Soup With Shirataki Noodles- Lectin Free

Serves: 2
Cooking Time: 15 minutes
Preparation Time: 15 minutes

Ingredients

- Vegetable or Chicken Stock 28 oz plant paradox compliant
- Miracle Noodle capellini 1 bag
- Miso Paste 2 tbsp
- Cooked, sliced chicken breast 6 oz
- Shredded Green Cabbage 1 cup
- Bok Choi sliced half 2
- Coriander handful
- Raw peeled carrot 1 small
- Few scallions
- Salt and pepper as per taste

Preparation

1. Look at the pack of the noodles for cooking instructions. Follow these instructions carefully for better taste.
2. Take a bow, add the stock along with the shredded cabbage. You need to boil it for 7 minutes and then add sliced chicken, bok choi and simmer it for 3-4 minutes.

3. Turn off the heat, and then add the miso paste. Now mix everything well. You can add more miso paste if you want.
4. Take two serving bowls and add the noodles in them. After that add chicken to oil bowls, coriander, scallions, carrot ribbons, and bok choi.
5. You can save the soup for a day in your fridge.

Romanian Style Beef Soup

Serves: 6
Cooking time 2 hours
Preparation Time: 40 minutes.

Ingredients

- Water
- Salt as per taste
- Peeled, cubed Japanese sweet potato 1 medium
- Sour cream 4 tbsp (optional)
- Pastured egg yolk 1-2 (optional)
- Chopped parsley 1 bunch
- Chopped celery leaves 1 handful
- Sauerkraut with juice 1 cup or to taste
- Peeled and chopped parsnip 1 medium
- Peeled or chopped celery root ½ big
- Peeled and chopped carrot 1 big
- Bone broth 28 oz
- Cut in bite pieces Grass-fed beef 1-1.5 lbs

Preparation

1. Take a big bowl; add complaint broth or stock and meat pieces in water. Bring the mixture to boiling, then remove the foam. After this throw away the water, wash the meat and the soup pot. Restart the process with bone broth and end it with cold water.
2. Prepare onion, celery root, parsnip, and carrots during the time the meat is boiling. Chop all these vegetables in small cubes, also try to make all these cubes even.
3. Chop the sweet potatoes as well, but they are to be slightly bigger than other vegetables.

4. Chop broccoli in small pieces and wait till the end to chop celery and parsley leaves.
5. Once the meat is almost done add sweet potato, parsnip, celery root, onion, and carrots. Allow low heat to boil everything. This will take about 30-40 minutes. Finally add sauerkraut along with parsley leaves, celery leaves, and broccoli. Add salt as per your taste.
6. In case you want to add sour cream and egg to the soup. Whisk them well and slowly add some hot soup to the mix. Once the mix is warm itself, you can add it to the soup pot.

Okra Stew With Green Cabbage- Lectin-Free

Serves: 3-4
Cooking Time: 30-40 minutes
Preparation Time: 15 minutes

Ingredients

Cabbage Salad Ingredients

- Apple Cider Vinegar to taste
- Extra virgin oil olive as per taste
- Pepper and salt as per taste
- Finely shredded green cabbage ½

Okra Stew Ingredients

- Extra virgin olive oil
- Pepper and salt as per taste
- Vegetable, chicken or compliant stock 1 cup
- Bay leaf 1
- Cumin powder 1 Tsp
- Coriander powder 1 Tsp
- Smoked paprika 1 tsp
- Organic Hungarian paprika 2 tsp
- Garlic Cloves 3
- Chopped red onion 1 medium
- Washed and dried fresh okra 1 QT

Preparation

For Okra Stew:

1. Chop the okra stems in about ½ inch pieces.

2. Take a stew pan and add olive oil in it. Heat it a bit and then add chopped red onion. Cook them on medium heat until they are translucent.
3. Now add bay leaf, coriander, cumin, paprika, chopped garlic, and chopped okra. Stir and cook everything for about 5-8 minutes.
4. Turn the heat to low medium and slowly add the stock to it. The adding to stock will take about 30 minutes. By the time you have added all the stock, okra will be ready.

For Cabbage Salad

1. Add salt to the finely chopped cabbage and massage it with your hands. Keep massaging until no moisture is left.
2. Now add salt, pepper to taste, apple cider and olive oil. That is it, your cabbage salad is ready.

Vegan Coriander And Lime Cauliflower Rice- Lectin Free

Serves: 1-2 person
Cooking Time: 5 minutes
Preparation Time: 5 minutes

Ingredients

- Organic ground black pepper 1 tsp
- Himalayan pink salt 1 Tsp
- Pure avocado oil 1 tbsp
- Organic lime-juice 2 tbsp
- Organic cauliflower rice 2 cup

For add-in

- Organic and Fresh coriander ¼ cup

Preparation

1. Take a skillet and add all the ingredients in it. Saute it for about 5 minutes until you get a consistency that you like. You can add or remove seasonings; it all depends on your taste.
2. Remove the heat and then add the coriander. Make sure that it is evenly distributed.
3. You can garnish it with extra chopped coriander and serve it.

Vegan Shirataki Angel Hair Pasta With Creamy Chipotle Avocado Sauce- Lectin Free

Serves: 2
Cooking time: 5 minutes
Preparation time: 5 minutes

Ingredients

- Shirataki Angel Hair Pasta 2 packs

For sauce
- Himalayan pink salt ¼ to ½ tsp
- Organic ground chipotle powder ½ - 1 Tsp
- Organic lime juice 2 tbsp
- Organic avocados 2

Preparation

Read the instruction on the package to prepare the pasta.

For the Sauce

1. Take a Vitamix and add all the ingredients to it. Blend everything well until you get a smooth and creamy mixture.
2. You can adjust the seasonings according to your taste.

Preparation

1. Take a bowl and transfer the pasta into it.
2. Add the sauce to the pasta and toss it for even distribution of the sauce.

Vegan Mushroom Cauliflower Rice Risotto- Lectin Free

Serves: 1-2
Cooking Time: 10 minutes
Preparation Time 10 minutes

Ingredients

- Organic ground sage ½ Tsp
- Organic ground black pepper 1 tsp
- Himalayan pink salt 1 Tsp
- Organic extra-virgin olive oil 2 tbsp
- Organic garlic cloves 2 (freshly crushed)
- Diced Organic red onion ½ cup
- Diced organic baby Bella mushrooms 1 ½ cup

For add-ins

- Organic cauliflower rice
- Organic full-fat coconut milk 1 can (13.5 ounces)

Preparation

1. Put the coconut milk in the refrigerator overnight.
2. Take a skillet and add all the ingredients excluding coconut milk and cauliflower rice. Heat should be medium-high, sauté the ingredients until both the onions and the mushrooms turn soft.
3. Now remove the can from the refrigerator and add only the hard top layer, coconut fat. Do not add the liquid layer underneath as this will reduce the thickness of the risotto.
4. When you are adding coconut fat, at the same time add cauliflower rice as well. Stir all these things together.

5. Turn heat to medium and simmer until cauliflower rice turns soft. That is it, take it out and serve it.

Drinks And Smoothies

Avocado Smoothie Bowl

Serves: 1
Cooking Time: 10 minutes
Preparation time: 5 minutes

Ingredients

- Extra virgin Olive Oil 1 tbsp
- Salt 1 pinch medium
- Liquid stevia ¼ Tsp
- Vanilla extract ¼ tsp
- Matcha 1 tsp (optional)
- Erythritol 1 tbsp
- Flax meal 1 ½ tbsp
- Full fat coconut milk ¼ c along with 2 tbsp (3 oz)
- Ripe avocado meat 1 large (3 oz)

Topping

- Fresh blueberries
- Crushed pistachios
- Toasted coconut flakes

Preparation

1. Take a mini food processor and put all the ingredients. Bleed everything until you get a smooth consistency.
2. You might have to pause the blending, shake the smoothie and blend it again.
3. In case you find it think, you can add a little water to it. Now sprinkle any or all topping to add taste.

Classic Hot Chocolate

Serves: 2
Cooking time: 10 minutes
Preparation time: 5 minutes

Ingredients

- Sea salt ¼ tsp
- Liquid stevia extract ½ tsp
- Vanilla extract 1 tsp
- Virgin coconut oil 1tbsp
- Cocoa powder 20 g
- Light coconut milk 3 cups

Preparation

1. Take a food processor and add all salt, stevia, vanilla, coconut oil, cocoa powder and one cup of coconut milk. Blend it for about 10 seconds.
2. Now take a medium saucepan to add the chocolate mixture to it and heat it over high heat. Now slowly add the remaining coconut oil and simmer it well.
3. Divide the drink into two cups and enjoy it.

Avo Nog

Serves: 3 glasses
Time: 15 minutes

Ingredients

- Rum, bourbon, or whiskey (optional)
- Cinnamon ¼ tsp
- Vanilla extract ½ tsp
- Ground nutmeg ¾ tsp
- Erythritol or Xylitol ¼ c
- Aquafaba ½ cc
- Full fat coconut milk 1 can (13.5 oz)
- Ripe avocado 1 medium size.

Preparation

- To make sure that the drink is of enjoyable temperature by the time it is ready to serve, use chilled aquafaba, coconut oil and avocado.
- Take a medium bowl with an electric whisk and add aquafaba to the bowl. Beat on high speed until you can see medium peaks. This will take about 5 minutes.
- Now take a mini food processor and blend erythritol or xylitol, cinnamon, vanilla, nutmeg, avocado, and coconut milk together. Keep blending until you get a smooth mixture.
- Now put this mixture into aquafaba and stir until you can't see aquafaba anymore.
- If you desire, you can add whiskey at this point. Start with 3 tablespoons and add as per desire. 4

Sauces And Sweet Bites

Warm Ginger Bread In A Mug

Serves: 1
Cooking Time: 7 minutes
Preparation Time: 5 minutes

Ingredients

- Lightly beaten egg 1
- Water ½ tbsp.
- Apple cider vinegar ½ tsp
- Maple-flavored erythritol syrup 2 Tsp
- Baking powder ½ tsp
- Nutmeg, cloves, allspice pinch each
- Cinnamon ¼ tsp
- Ground ginger ½ tsp
- Cassava flour or tiger nut 1 tbsp
- Coconut flour 1 tbsp
- Softened butter 1 tbsp

Preparation

1. Take a microwave safe mug and add allspice, cinnamon, ginger, tiger nut flour, coconut flour and butter to it. Beat all these things together.
2. After beating, them properly mix in egg, cider vinegar, and syrup and beat vigorously with a fork. Beat until the batter is smooth.
3. Put the mug in a microwave for 1 ½ minute. Scrape the edges and enjoy the amazing muffin.
4. You can even top it with butter and cinnamon.

www.ingramcontent.com/pod-product-compliance
Lightning Source LLC
Chambersburg PA
CBHW071437070526
44578CB00001B/116